Sexual Harassment in Higher Education:
From Conflict to Community

by Robert O. Riggs, Patricia H. Murrell, and JoAnn C. Cutting

ASHE-ERIC Higher Education Report No. 2, 1993

Prepared by

Clearinghouse on Higher Education
The George Washington University

In cooperation with

Association for the Study
of Higher Education

Published by

School of Education and Human Development
The George Washington University

Jonathan D. Fife, Series Editor

Cite as

Riggs, Robert O., Patricia H. Murrell, and JoAnn C. Cutting. 1993. *Sexual Harassment in Higher Education: From Conflict to Community.* ASHE-ERIC Higher Education Report No. 2. Washington, D.C.: The George Washington University, School of Education and Human Development.

Library of Congress Catalog Card Number 93-86308
ISSN 0884-0040
ISBN 1-878380-23-0

Managing Editor: Bryan Hollister
Manuscript Editor: Alexandra Rockey
Cover design by Michael David Brown, Rockville, Maryland

The ERIC Clearinghouse on Higher Education invites individuals to submit proposals for writing monographs for the *ASHE-ERIC Higher Education Report* series. Proposals must include:
1. A detailed manuscript proposal of not more than five pages.
2. A chapter-by-chapter outline.
3. A 75-word summary to be used by several review committees for the initial screening and rating of each proposal.
4. A vita and a writing sample.

ERIC Clearinghouse on Higher Education
School of Education and Human Development
The George Washington University
One Dupont Circle, Suite 630
Washington, DC 20036-1183

This publication was prepared partially with funding from the Office of Educational Research and Improvement, U.S. Department of Education, under contract no. ED RI-88-062014. The opinions expressed in this report do not necessarily reflect the positions or policies of OERI or the Department.

EXECUTIVE SUMMARY

Colleges and universities are expected to provide learning and working environments wherein all members of academic communities may pursue their studies, scholarship, and work without bias or intimidation. The specter of sexual harassment is inimical to this end.

Since the impact and scope of the sexual harassment problem on college campuses first were recognized during the early 1980s, an enormous amount of attention has been focused on the problem. Campuses have developed policies, procedures, extensive training programs, and materials that seek to identify and prevent sexual harassment and promoted conferences and symposia addressing the problem. Yet, in spite of these substantial initiatives and perhaps as a result of heightened awareness of sexual harassment as a problem (or perhaps more people alleging harassment), the frequency of complaints on college and university campuses has increased (Leatherman 1992).

What Is the Definition of Sexual Harassment and Why Is It Illegal?

Unwelcome sexual advances, requests for sexual favors, and other verbal or physical conduct of a sexual nature constitute sexual harassment when (1) submission to such conduct is made explicitly or implicitly a term or condition of an individual's employment; (2) submission to or rejection of such conduct by an individual is used as a basis for employment decisions affecting such an individual; or (3) such conduct has the purpose or effect of unreasonably interfering with an individual's work performance or creating an intimidating, hostile, or offensive working environment (American Council on Education 1986).

Sexual harassment is a form of sexual discrimination and is prohibited by federal laws. Title VII of the Civil Rights Act of 1964 and Title IX of the Education Amendments of 1972 are the federal statutes under which are brought the majority of sexual harassment complaints against higher education institutions and their employees. The Civil Rights Act of 1991 provides additional rights and remedies to sexual harassment complainants.

What Kinds of Behavior Constitute Sexual Harassment?

Sexually harassing behaviors encompass a broad range of actions, including unwelcome sexual advances or requests for sexual favors when the acceptance or rejection of such actions serves as a basis for academic or employment decisions. Sexual harassment behavior also includes conduct that interferes with a student's or employee's performance by allowing the existence of a hostile working or learning environment.

More specifically, sexually harassing behavior includes the following: (1) gender harassment, including sexist statements and behavior that convey insulting, degrading, or sexist attitudes; (2) seductive behavior encompassing unwanted, inappropriate, and offensive physical or verbal sexual advances; (3) sexual bribery, involving solicitation of sexual activity or other sex-linked behavior by promise of reward; (4) sexual coercion of sexual activity or other sex-linked behavior by threat of punishment; and (5) sexual assault, attempted rape, and rape (Fitzgerald et al. 1988).

How Often Does Sexual Harassment Occur on Campuses, and Who Are the Victims?

While all members of the academic community are potential victims of unwelcome sexual behavior, the majority of complainants are female students, faculty, and staff. Dziech and Weiner reported that 20 to 30 percent of undergraduate female students are the victims of some form of sexual harassment by at least one of their professors during their undergraduate years (1984), and Ernest Boyer reported that more than 60 percent of the presidents surveyed at large research and doctorate institutions said sexual harassment is a problem (1990).

When the definition of harassment is expanded to include sexist remarks and other forms of gender harassment, the incidence rate among undergraduate women exceeds 75 percent (Adams, Kotke, and Padgitt 1983). Fitzgerald et al. reported approximately 50 percent of women at one university and nearly 76 percent at another university indicated that they had experienced some form of harassing behavior during their careers (1988). Paludi and Barickman suggest that, because of power structures and cultural biases within the academy, women are overwhelmingly the targets of sexual harassment and, although a profile has not been empirically established, nearly all harassers are male (1991c).

What Steps Should Institutions Take to Eliminate Sexual Harassment From the Academy?

Members of institutional boards of governance and college and university administrators must provide strong support to programs to eliminate sexual harassment if this blight is to be removed from the academy. Among the most important steps that institutional leaders must take to this end are: (1) carefully drafted definitions of what constitutes sexual harassment and clear policies that prohibit such actions; (2) accessible grievance procedures that are communicated to and understood by all members of the academic community; and (3) ongoing efforts to educate the campus community about the nature of sexual harassment and its destructive impact within the community. Taken together, these three steps represent the best practice that institutions have experienced after more than a decade of aggressive response to the problem.

From Conflict to Community
The nation's colleges and universities occupy roles in our culture that impose unique expectations and opportunities. They are obligated to serve as moral exemplars by embracing diversity and inclusiveness while providing an environment free of debilitating harassment. They must lead by example in eliminating gender inequities among all segments of the academic community. They have also the important opportunity to shape the future by forging an ethos of enfranchisement, equity, and care. In no other institution in American society are these expectations and opportunities more clearly focused than in institutions of higher education.

ADVISORY BOARD

CONSULTING EDITORS

Louis C. Attinasi, Jr.
University of Houston

Beverly Belson
Western Michigan University

David W. Breneman
Harvard University

Kimberly Brown
Portland State University

L. Edwin Coate
Oregon State University

Elsa Kircher Cole
The University of Michigan

Robert Cope
Northwoods Institute

Jane F. Earley
Mankato State University

Walter H. Gmelch
Washington State University

Dennis E. Gregory
Wake Forest University

James O. Hammons
University of Arkansas

Robert M. Hendrickson
The Pennsylvania State University

Mary Ann Heverly
Delaware County Community College

Malcolm D. Hill
The Pennsylvania State University

Clifford P. Hooker
University of Minnesota

George D. Kuh
Indiana University

Sock-Foon C. MacDougall
Bowie State University

James L. Morrison
The University of North Carolina–Chapel Hill

REVIEW PANEL

Charles Adams
University of Massachusetts-Amherst

Louis Albert
American Association for Higher Education

Richard Alfred
University of Michigan

Philip G. Altbach
State University of New York-Buffalo

Marilyn J. Amey
University of Kansas

Louis C. Attinasi, Jr.
University of Houston-University Park

Robert J. Barak
Iowa State Board of Regents

Alan Bayer
Virginia Polytechnic Institute and State University

John P. Bean
Indiana University-Bloomington

Louis W. Bender
The Florida State University

John M. Braxton
Vanderbilt University

Peter McE. Buchanan
Council for Advancement and
    Support of Education

John A. Centra
Syracuse University

Arthur W. Chickering
George Mason University

Shirley M. Clark
Oregon State System of Higher Education

Darrel A. Clowes
Virginia Polytechnic Institute and State University

John W. Creswell
University of Nebraska-Lincoln

Deborah DiCroce
Piedmont Virginia Community College

Richard Duran
University of California–Santa Barbara

Kenneth C. Green
University of Southern California

Edward R. Hines
Illinois State University

Marsha V. Krotseng
West Virginia State College and University Systems

George D. Kuh
Indiana University–Bloomington

Daniel T. Layzell
University of Wisconsin System

Meredith Ludwig
American Association of State Colleges and Universities

Mantha V. Mehallis
Florida Atlantic University

Robert J. Menges
Northwestern University

Toby Milton
Essex Community College

James R. Mingle
State Higher Education Executive Officers

Gary Rhoades
University of Arizona

G. Jeremiah Ryan
Harford Community College

Mary Ann Sagaria
Ohio State University

Daryl G. Smith
Claremont Graduate School

William Tierney
The Pennsylvania State University

Susan Twombly
University of Kansas

Harold S. Wechsler
University of Rochester

Michael J. Worth
The George Washington University

CONTENTS

FOREWORD

In the not too distant past, what many people considered sexual harassment and how they identified good art had a lot in common: "I don't know how to define it, but I know it when I see it." The problem was that what most people saw was not dependent on what was really occurring—but what such people did or did not want to see.

As psychological research confirms, beliefs play a major role in how people perceive their reality. In the male-dominated bastions of our society, it was believed that sexual harassment primarily was the product of some insecure female's mind. Today, this position not only is morally unacceptable, but it also is illegal. In other words, times have changed. If an organization does not make the issue of sexual harassment a major concern, the results could be very costly.

The first problem lies in defining sexual harassment. One element of the definition is easy: Sexual harassment is an act that uses coercion to force a person to perform a sexual favor against his or her will. But today, this type of blatant sexual harassment constitutes only part of what is considered sexually offensive and potentially illegal. Off-color jokes, derogatory names, sexually revealing pictures, casual hand gestures, and unwelcome touching are just some of the behaviors that can be interpreted as sexual harassment. As the cultural norms change, there is a confusion about what qualifies as appropriate behavior. Such confusion needs to be of concern to an organization because of the difficulty in monitoring sexual harassment.

Many aspects of sexual harassment make it very difficult—if not impossible—to control: The act usually occurs in private, often no hard evidence exists that could be presented in a hearing, and what has happened is subject to different interpretations. Therefore, organizations must be proactive in establishing guidelines of what is considered acceptable behavior and what behavior will not be tolerated. The effectiveness of the policy will depend on the degree to which the beliefs of the organization's members agree with the organization's sexual harassment policies. Most of the time this agreement can be reached only if an effort is made to sustain a face-to-face dialogue on why specific behavior is perceived to be acceptable or unacceptable.

Such direct action to change or reinforce organizational cultural values must be consistent, or it will not work. Consistency depends on common knowledge and understanding of the issue. In this report, Robert O. Riggs, regents professor at the Center for the Study of Higher Education, Patricia H. Murrell, director of the Center for the Study of Higher Education, and JoAnn C. Cutting, assistant general counsel for the University of Tennesse, have contributed greatly to developing this common understanding. After defining the legal nature of sexual harassment, they look at the many ways it has been experienced at higher education institutions. They follow this discussion with an examination of how institutions have addressed this issue. Finally, the authors look at the specific actions that individuals and activities must take to eliminate sexual harassment.

Sexual harassment is more than just a moral, legal, or financial concern. It is a concern over protecting an atmosphere that is most conducive to our academic ideals. In a condition of fear or emotional discomfort, academic goals cannot be achieved. In an organization where faculty are protected from direct supervision by tenure and academic freedom, ensuring that the organizational culture promotes beliefs and values that makes sexual harassment unlikely to exist is additionally important. This report will be very useful to higher education institutions as they address this critical issue.

Jonathan D. Fife, Series Editor
Professor of Higher Education Administration and
Director, ERIC Clearinghouse on Higher Education

ACKNOWLEDGMENTS

The authors wish to convey their appreciation to the colleagues who contributed to the development of this report. They include Ricci Hellman of the Memphis Sexual Abuse Center; Judy Chencharick of the University of Tennessee Center for Health Sciences; Pat Morris of Union University; and Bill Nourse, Olivia Wilson, and Lucy Williford of Memphis State University, Center for the Study of Higher Education.

THE LEGAL CONTEXT OF SEXUAL HARASSMENT

Anita Hill, Clarence Thomas, Tailhook, Senator Bob Packwood, *Franklin v. Gwinnett,* Judge David Lanier.

Each of these names, events, or incidents reported in the news helped to propel the topic of sexual harassment to the fore in the thinking of the American public. They also exemplify the complex, pervasive, and, at times, insidious nature of the problem.

While none of these highly publicized incidents specifically involved higher education, the literature clearly indicates that colleges and universities have experienced their share of problems and are not immune to the resulting loss of public confidence—or to the damage to human potential and productivity. Indeed, the presence of students adds a dimension not found in other settings. The hierarchical nature of the relationship between learners and teachers in most educational situations creates a delicate and fragile imbalance of power where the development of trust is essential and where students may be especially vulnerable. That higher education's experiences have not been sufficiently sensational to merit national headlines and evening newscasts is probably due less to their seriousness and importance than to the relatively low national recognition of those involved.

Such harassment is a form of sex or gender discrimination.

This report presents the bases and origins of sexual harassment from the perspective of both statutes and prominent court cases. It identifies behaviors involved in sexual harassment, examines the prevalence of the problem in higher education, and explores institutional responses in terms of policies and procedures. Finally, it urges colleges and universities to move toward an environment in which the imbalance of power and innate structural inequalities are ameliorated—one in which an ethic of care and responsibility replaces a culture of dependence and inherent inequality.

Terminology on the topic of sexual harassment in the literature has evolved. For example, Franklin et al. draw a distinction between sexual and gender harassment (1981); however, the law on which this discussion is based refers to sexual harassment. Thus, that is the predominant language of this report. Consequently, where the term *gender harassment* appears, it is used synonymously with *sexual harassment.* The term *sexual harassment* will be used throughout this report to encompass a range of illegal and unethical behaviors ranging from gender harassment to sexual imposition.

Fitzgerald et al. provide the following classification of sexual harassment:

- Gender harassment: Generalized sexist statements and behavior that convey insulting, degrading, and/or sexist attitudes;
- Seductive behavior: Unwanted, inappropriate, and offensive physical or verbal sexual advances;
- Sexual bribery: Solicitation of sexual activity or other sex-linked behavior by promise of reward;
- Sexual coercion: Coercion of sexual activity or other sex-linked behavior by threat of punishment; and
- Sexual assault: Assault and/or rape (1988, pp. 152-75).

Throughout this manuscript, *sexual harassment* is used as an inclusive term as proposed by Fitzgerald.

Institutions of higher education constitute a major source of employment for thousands of individuals in America and provide educational experiences for many more. Colleges and universities are required to afford equal opportunities to employees and students regardless of race, sex, age, or national origin. An individual may sue the institution or its employees for violation of her or his civil rights pursuant to legislation that ensures the protection of these rights. These statutes, and the body of case law that has developed interpreting them, have had and continue to have a profound impact on the way educational institutions conduct the business of education.

What Is Sexual or Gender Harassment?
Stated briefly, sexual harassment includes the demands for sexual favors in exchange for benefits (*quid pro quo*) or the creation of a hostile work or educational environment (*Meritor Savings Bank FSB v. Vinson* 1986). Such harassment is a form of sex or gender discrimination—one of a group of civil rights violations against which all institutions must guard. An expanded definition of sexual harassment, first promulgated in the Equal Employment Opportunity Commission (EEOC) guidelines in 1980 and later adopted by the Supreme Court in *Meritor Savings Bank FSB v. Vinson* (1986), is as follows:

> "*[u]nwelcome sexual advances, requests for sexual favors, and other verbal or physical conduct of a sexual nature . . . when (1) submission to such conduct is made either*

*explicitly or implicitly a term or condition of an individual's
employment, (2) submission to or rejection of such conduct
by an individual is used as the basis for employment decisions affecting such individual, or (3) such conduct has
the purpose or effect of unreasonably interfering with an
individual's work performance or creating an intimidating,
hostile, or offensive working environment."*

Harassers and victims may be male or female, and sexual
harassment may exist between or among people of the same
sex. The harasser may be a victim's supervisor, co-worker,
agent of the victim's employer, or a non-employee (e.g., an
independent contractor, customer, agent, or consultant of the
employer). Anyone affected by the harassment—not just the
person against whom the conduct is directed—could have
a valid complaint. In other words, colleagues who find an
unwelcome hostile environment may object, even if the
harasser's actions are not directed toward them (EEOC 1992).

How Has the Law Developed Relative to Members of
the Academic Community?
Sexual harassment became the object of considerable attention beginning in the 1970s and received heightened attention
with the highly publicized confirmation hearings of U.S.
Supreme Court Justice Clarence Thomas. The EEOC reported
that the number of complaints it received in the first quarter
of 1992 was up 41 percent over those filed during that same
period in 1991 (Affirmative Action Compliance Manual 1992).
In addition, the passage of the Civil Rights Act of 1991 allowing for jury trials and the recovery of additional monetary
damages for victims, as well as the Supreme Court finding
that students may recover under Title IX of the Educational
Amendments of 1972 monetary damages for sexual harassment (*Franklin v. Gwinnett Co. Public Schools* 1992), make
it imperative for college and university officials to understand
this subject.

While the law that deals explicitly with the sexual harassment of students is less developed than that applied in cases
involving employees, courts appear to be adopting the same
general legal reasoning for both. A significant number of legal
principles has developed that apply to educational institutions,
their employees, and students.

The two federal statutes under which the vast majority of sexual discrimination claims are brought against higher education institutions or their employees are Title VII of the Civil Rights Act of 1964 as amended and Title IX of the Education Amendments of 1972. Aggrieved employees of an institution normally allege violations of Title VII (which is enforced by the EEOC) while students seek relief under Title IX law, which is monitored by the United States Office of Civil Rights (OCR). While neither the EEOC nor the OCR has adjudicatory powers, both agencies receive and investigate complaints, effectuate conciliation agreements, and make determinations of whether harassment has occurred.

Title VII

The Civil Rights Act of 1964—originally intended to protect African Americans from racial discrimination—was expanded just before its passage by Congress to include gender discrimination and thus harassment as well (Clark 1991). Colleges and universities as entities, as well as their employees, are subject to Title VII, which states in part that, ". . . it is an unlawful employment practice for an employer . . . to discriminate against an individual with respect to . . . [the] terms, conditions or privileges of employment, because of the individual['s] . . . sex . . ." (Civil Rights Act of 1964). As employers, institutions of higher learning must not make employment decisions based on gender during the initial recruitment and hiring process or during the subsequent period of an individual's employment. Thus, under Title VII, colleges or universities as entities and their employees as well as agents or independent contractors of the institution may have liability if they engage in acts of harassment (EEOC 1992).

In addition to making sex discrimination unlawful, the Civil Rights Act of 1964 also created the EEOC to handle complaints filed pursuant to the statute. Originally vested with limited investigational powers, the EEOC was given expanded authority in 1972 pursuant to the Equal Employment Opportunity Act (Clark 1991). This authority includes the right to settle complaints between the charging party and the employer, to sue the employer on behalf of the complainant, or, in the case of an employer that is a state institution, to refer the case to the U.S. Attorney General for possible legal action (Civil Rights Act of 1964).

Since its inception, the EEOC has published guidelines relative to sexual or gender harassment, many of which have been cited with approval by courts, including the Supreme Court (such as *Meritor Savings Bank* 1986; *Franklin* 1992). In 1990, the Commission issued substantially expanded guidelines that are available from the EEOC, along with other general information. The information may be obtained by contacting the Office of Communications and Legislative Affairs, EEOC, 1801 L St., N.W., Washington, D.C. 20507; (800) 669-EEOC.

Title VII Court Cases
Initially, trial courts were reluctant to recognize the applicability of Title VII to unwelcome sexual advances *(Corne v. Bausch and Lomb, Inc.* 1975). However, in the late 1970s, judges began to uphold causes of action brought under this statute (NEA 1992, citing *Barnes v. Castle* 1977; *Tomkins v. Public Service Electric* 1977). Finally, the Supreme Court in 1987 decided *Meritor Savings Bank FSB v. Vinson,* the case that conclusively determined that Title VII made illegal both *quid pro quo* and hostile environment sexual harassment. When the Supreme Court decided the *Meritor Bank* case, its opinion provided guidance to employers such as educational institutions regarding sexual harassment as a form of sexual discrimination.

In the *Meritor Bank* case, Vinson, a female, was offered a job by Taylor, a male bank branch manager. She progressed rapidly from her entry-level position into a management job, granting her supervisor, Taylor, sexual favors during a substantial part of her initial four years of employment. She subsequently denied his requests, went on indefinite sick leave, and was fired two months later—allegedly for abuse of the bank's sick-leave policy.

Vinson sued employee Taylor individually and the employer bank for sexual harassment under Title VII. She claimed constructive discharge resulting from sexual harassment by her supervisor; that is, the employer's actions—sexual harassment—created a work environment so intolerable that it forced her to be absent from the workplace and hence to be dismissed for abuse of sick-leave policy.

During the trial, Vinson testified that Taylor had begun requesting sexual favors shortly after she went to work at the bank. She claimed that while she initially refused his advances, she ultimately submitted to his requests. Taylor denied the accusations. The defendant bank also took the position that no harassment had occurred, but argued that if it had occurred it was without the knowledge and approval of the bank's officials (*Meritor* 1986).

Meritor Applications

While procedural questions kept the Supreme Court from reaching a final determination on the merits of Vinson's claims, the *Meritor* court did provide educational institutions with several helpful guidelines. These judicial pronouncements have been developed further by 1990 EEOC guidelines that provide additional assistance for avoiding harassment claims.

First, the Supreme Court recognized two forms of discriminatory sexual harassment: obtaining, improving the status of, or retaining employment in return for sexual favors, and interfering with an employee's work environment with conduct of a sexual nature, thus creating a hostile work environment.

Second, the court decided that ". . . not all workplace conduct that may be described as 'harassment' affects a Title VII aspect of employment. For sexual harassment to be actionable, it must be sufficiently severe or pervasive to alter the conditions of [the victim's] employment and create an abusive working environment" (*Meritor* 1986, p. 2,405). In all likelihood, a single sexual event would be sufficient to support a finding of *quid pro quo* sexual harassment if it were linked to hiring, advancement, or firing of an employee, or if it were determinative of the progress or promotion of a student. A significant physical event also would be sufficient to support such a claim. Less significant events would have to occur more frequently for such a determination to be made. Thus, a single incident, unless it is an especially egregious *quid pro quo* event, generally is not sufficient to allow a complainant to prevail in a sexual harassment lawsuit (EEOC 1990).

Third, the *Meritor* court noted that the appropriate question to be answered relative to a hostile environment harassment claim is whether the claimant's ". . . conduct indicated that the alleged sexual advances were unwelcome" (*Meritor* 1986, p. 2,406). Obviously sexual behavior, if welcome, is not unlawful (EEOC 1990). To be considered unwelcome conduct, actions or words must not have been actively solicited by the employee or must be considered "undesirable or offensive" to that individual. Hostile environment conduct must have "unreasonably interfered with . . . work performance" or created "an intimidating, hostile, or offensive work environment. The correct inquiry is whether the victim by his/her conduct indicated that the . . . advance was unwelcome, not whether . . . participation . . . was voluntary" *(Meritor* 1986, p. 2,406).

Several other facts may be considered but are not determinative of whether harassment has occurred. These include voluntary participation by the complainant, "provocative speech or dress," and whether the complainant informed the harasser that her or his behavior was offensive and requested that the behavior be stopped *(Meritor* 1986).

Fourth, the totality of the circumstances for each case should be carefully considered when evaluating complaints. The totality of the circumstances normally is judged by the reasonable person standard; however, a new test may be developing for determining unwelcome or offensive behavior. The "reasonable woman" standard has been recently adopted by several courts (Clark 1991, citing *Ellison v. Bailey).* (See also *Andrews v. City of Philadelphia* and *Lipsett v. University of Puerto Rico,* 864 F.2d 881 [1st Cir. 1988].) This gender-conscious measurement is thought to be more responsive to what may be considered offensive to each sex.

Fifth, the *Meritor* court provided guidelines to employers regarding employer liability in cases of alleged harassment. While declining to enunciate a specific rule on this issue, the court did adopt the position that employees may be agents of the employer. Thus, an employer may be liable even though it has no knowledge or notice of the harassment; however, liability is not automatically imputed merely as the result of an employee's acts of harassment. Courts would be required to apply the facts in each case to the general rule that employers act through their employees and that employees are agents of the employer *(Meritor* 1986).

In further developing the concept of institutional liability, courts have continued to suggest that allegations must first be divided into either *quid pro quo* or hostile environment claims before an appropriate analysis of liability can be executed. The EEOC in its 1990 guidelines concluded that, in cases of *quid pro quo* harassment, "an employer will almost always [be] responsible for the acts of a supervisor because the supervisor is making decisions that directly affect a specific condition of the victim's employment" (EEOC 1990). Under EEOC's analysis, supervisors act as agents of the employer and within their employer's delegated authority, even when they initiate an illegal harassing action. Thus, *quid pro quo* harassment likely will be imputed to the employer. In contrast, an employer is less likely to be held liable in hostile environment cases unless someone at a higher supervisory level—or an officer or director—knew or should have known of the harassment and refused to take action to correct the inappropriate behavior of the employee (EEOC 1990).

Finally, the *Meritor* court found that an institution may be liable even if it has an internal policy addressing harassment. The Meritor Bank had a broad anti-discrimination policy and an internal grievance procedure, yet the court did not look favorably upon the bank's failure to specifically address gender harassment in that policy. This failure was cited as evidencing the employer's apparent lack of dedication to dealing with complaints from victims in this area. Furthermore, the court was not impressed by the bank's procedure requiring Vinson to first complain to her supervisor pursuant to the broad anti-discrimination policy, since her supervisor was the alleged harasser. However, Vinson's failure to file an internal complaint was considered to be an important fact in the employer bank's favor *(Meritor* 1986).

The most recent EEOC guidelines indicate that the employer will be liable for its employees' actions if it has no policy against sexual harassment and no procedure for victims to complain and obtain relief. In addition, failure to communicate the policy to all employees also may create liability (EEOC 1990). Thus, an employer's best protection against incurring such liability rests first in having a strong anti-harassment policy with its procedures clearly conveyed to all employees and, second, in taking prompt corrective action if harassing behavior occurs.

Title IX

The Meritor Bank case and EEOC publications form a framework for the educational institution in dealing with its employees and their potential sexual harassment complaints. Federal laws and an equally important case, *Franklin v. Gwin-*

nett Co. Public Schools and Hill, provide guidance for colleges and universities for addressing student claims.

Educational institutions that receive federal assistance are subject to Title IX of the Education Amendments of 1972. This law provides in pertinent part that "[n]o person . . . shall, on the basis of sex, be excluded from participation in . . . benefits of, or be subjected to discrimination under any educational program or activity receiving federal financial assistance. . . ." Under this statute, institutions as well as staff, students, and faculty may be liable for sexual harassment claims brought by students.

Just as employees were not successful in early Title VII claims, students who sued under Title IX experienced difficulties. Using Title IX as a basis, a female student at Yale sued her male professor when she received a course grade of "C" rather than "A." She claimed that the lower grade was the result of her refusal of the professor's sexual advances (*Alexander v. Yale* 1980). The *Yale* court determined that the student had been a victim of *quid pro quo* discrimination. However, no monetary damages were awarded, and the court left undecided the hostile environment theory as a valid basis for Title IX claims. Subsequently, the case was dismissed because the student graduated.

Other courts and ultimately the Supreme Court determined that students not only could sustain a cause of action under Title IX but also could recover monetary compensation. Any question as to whether a student alleging harassment could sue and recover monetary damages from an educational institution or an employee of that institution under Title IX was answered in the 1992 Supreme Court decision *Franklin v. Gwinnett Co. Public Schools and Hill.*

In *Franklin,* a high school student claimed she had been sexually harassed by a coach and teacher, Hill. Hill had begun a friendship with Franklin in 1986. He wrote her excuses for being late to class and allowed her to grade test papers for him. During the next two years, Hill requested and received sexual favors, including sexual intercourse, from Franklin. The band director, assistant principal, guidance counselor, and several teachers were told of Hill's actions. Finally, in February 1988, the school principal was informed. He discouraged Franklin's attempts to pursue a complaint and tried to influence her, through her boyfriend, not to take any action.

In March 1988, the Gwinnett County School Board began

its investigation into Franklin's allegations. When Hill resigned and the principal retired at year's end, the board closed its investigation without any final resolution of the complaint. Franklin filed a claim with the OCR, U.S. Department of Education. OCR investigated and found that while the Gwinnett County school system had violated Title IX, its assurance that it had taken affirmative action to prevent such behavior in the future was sufficient to avoid liability. OCR closed its investigation. Franklin then filed suit in federal court seeking monetary damages under Title IX of the Education Amendments of 1972 *(Franklin* 1990).

The Supreme Court found that the Gwinnett Co. Public Schools had a duty not to discriminate against its students on the basis of gender. Applying the general rule from Meritor Bank, the *Franklin* court held that "when a supervisor sexually harasses a subordinate because of the subordinate's sex, that supervisor discriminate[s] on the basis of sex" *(Franklin* 1992). In addition, the court determined that Franklin could maintain a Title IX case against Hill individually.

Title IX Applications

The law relative to student harassment is not as well developed as the legal guidance educational institutions have for similar problems involving employees. At a minimum, college and university faculty, staff, and administrators would do well to assume that the general legal concepts of employment discrimination also apply to student harassment. Colleges and universities are strongly advised to develop and publicize sexual harassment policies and procedures for employees; as a minimum, education institutions must take the same action for students. While the development of Title VII law strongly *suggests* the development of policies and procedures, Title IX law *requires* that institutions establish such documents. Additionally, information seminars on harassment are suggested for all members of the academic community (Clark 1991).

Because of the more pronounced vulnerability of students in teacher-pupil or staff-student relationships, courts are more likely to hold professors and institutions to a higher level of accountability than cases involving employer-employee sexual harassment claims (Schneider 1987). It appears that even tenure will not protect a faculty member found to have committed a serious offense of sexual harassment *(Levitt v. University of Texas, El Paso* 1985). Furthermore, consent by the student may not be a viable defense and a same-sex harassment case will not be dismissed based on that fact alone *(Korf v. Ball State University* 1984). At least one author has suggested that a "reasonable student" standard is appropriate for determining what constitutes harassment in cases involving students (Schneider 1987).

The Civil Rights Act of 1991

On November 21, 1991, the Civil Rights Act of 1991 was signed into law giving complainants in Title VII harassment cases additional potential damage awards when combined with the previously existing Title VII remedies. The law now provides for a jury trial to determine the possible payment of compensatory and punitive damages, back pay, front pay, reinstatement, and recovery of attorney and expert-witness fees. Compensatory damages are defined as ". . . future pecuniary losses, emotional pain, suffering, inconvenience, mental anguish, loss of enjoyment of life and other nonpecuniary losses." While there are legislatively prescribed limits on certain damages (e.g., state institutions are not subject to punitive damages), the possibility of a substantial recovery by a successful harassment complainant looms larger than ever. However, even prior to the passage of this act, judgment and settlements had on occasion exceeded $1 million (Clark 1991).

The Campus Sexual Assault Victims' Bill of Rights

The Campus Sexual Assault Victims' Bill of Rights (1992) provides yet another law with implications for educational institutions dealing with sexual harassment. This legislation requires all institutions of higher education participating in any program that utilizes federal funds to establish policies aimed at preventing sexual offenses. Institutions must develop a policy addressing the rights of sexual assault victims that will allow them to have reported assaults:

- treated seriously;
- investigated and perhaps adjudicated both criminally and civilly with the full cooperation of campus officials; and
- fully reported to authorities without pressure from school officials that the victims not do so and without suggestions that the victims somehow are responsible for the crimes.

It appears that even tenure will not protect a faculty member found to have committed a serious offense of sexual harassment.

In addition, the policy must reference the victims' rights to:

- the same assistance the institution furnishes the accused in disciplinary hearings;
- cooperation from school officials in obtaining evidence;
- information regarding state and federal laws addressing the testing of suspects for diseases and disclosure of the test results to the victim;
- counseling and psychiatric help;
- reasonable efforts by the administration to protect the victim from the alleged assailant; and
- habitability in campus housing that provides a living space free from intimidation or other disruptive behavior.

This law fails to specifically define sexual assault or sexual offense; consequently, institutional administrators will need to frame definitions and policies that comply with this act and that relate logically and effectively to campus sexual harassment policies, procedures, and prevention programs. One example of a well-coordinated response to this statute is found with The George Washington University Sexual Assault Crisis Consultation Team (1992).

Administrators also should be cognizant of the definitions of sexual assault and other sexual offenses delineated by the Federal Bureau of Investigation's Uniform Crime Reporting System (see 20 USC 1092 (f) (6); 668.48 (d) [3]).

State Statutes

Not only do complainants have federal laws prohibiting discrimination and permitting monetary recovery, but they also may rely on state statutes for expanded bases for recovery and increased damages. State tort laws, for example, may provide a way for harassment victims to win damages for pain and suffering. Some states also may have anti-discrimination statutes similar to Titles VII and IX, thus giving alleged victims additional options for filing suit. For example, the Tennessee Human Rights Act (1992) may be used for redress by employees in that state, while the California Sexual Harassment Statutes prohibiting such behavior in educational institutions (1992) may allow a cause of action to be brought by students in that state.

Against this complex legal backdrop we now move to the college and university environment in an effort to determine the specific behaviors involved in sexual harassment, its prevalence, its causes, and appropriate institutional response.

What Conduct Constitutes Sexual Harassment?

Though a basic definition of sexual harassment is essential to developing policies and procedures for handling complaints, Mary Rowe (1987), a pioneer in the field of sexual harassment, asserts that no two people seem to agree about what it is. There are at least as many definitions as there are people making the definitions. Biaggio, Watts, and Brownell further warn that "restrictive and technical definitions may not take into account more subtle and insidious forms of harassment" (1990). Whether an institution embraces a narrow or a broad definition and interpretation of sexual harassment will greatly affect the subsequent development of its policies and procedures.

As indicated earlier, the *Meritor Bank* case noted that the conduct must be "sufficiently severe or pervasive . . . to alter the conditions of [the harassed person's] employment and create an abusive working environment." In addition, the act must be unwelcome by the aggrieved person. Further, other courts have determined that "the amount and nature of the conduct" and the relationship between the parties must be considered within "the totality of the circumstances" (p. 2,406).

Additionally, an isolated incident does not seem to be a sufficient basis for maintaining legal action, and it is not so much the intent of the harasser that is in question but the way in which the harassment is perceived by the victim. Questionable conduct within this broad framework thus can run the gamut from sexist remarks to actual sexual assaults.

Perhaps the most commonly accepted definitions (American Council on Education 1986; Carleton College 1990; Paludi and Barickman 1991; American Association of University Professors 1990a) are those that parallel or encompass the wording of the EEOC guidelines cited earlier. The key words in this definition are "unwelcome," "discriminatory," and "offensive."

Some definitions describe examples of verbal, non-verbal, and physical harassment (Hughes and Sandler 1986). Verbal harassment may include sexual innuendoes, off-color jokes about sex or women in general, sexual propositions, implied or overt threats, and insulting sounds. Non-verbal harassment may include leering or ogling, making obscene gestures, and pornography. Examples of physical harassment include physical touching, patting, or pinching; attempted or actual kissing; and coerced sexual intercourse.

Though most definitions acknowledge that women may harass men and that same-sex harassment sometimes occurs, the vast majority of harassment cases involve men harassing women. Policies that make allowances for these broad definitions, examples, and categories will fit the needs of most institutions. Finally, while it is recognized that individuals may see sexual harassment differently, it is most prudent for institutional policies to adhere to a definition that does not stray too far from those accepted by the academic and legal communities.

Various campus groups have attempted to define sexual harassment in their policy statements for students. Words referring to sexual favors, advances, attention, and requests as "unwelcome," "offensive," "unwanted," "demeaning," and "degrading" are common and serve as reminders that the perception of the victim is paramount to the intent of the harasser. Other frequently cited behaviors are language, graphic material, physical contact of a sexual nature, threat, or coercion. Physical or verbal abuse of a sexual nature, including graphic commentaries about an individual's body, sexually degrading remarks used to describe an individual, or unwelcome propositions and physical advances of a sexual nature, also are found in some literature.

Some campus definitions also have been expanded to include the fact that sexual harassment results whenever acceptance or rejection of such sexual overtures becomes a condition of employment or academic standing; serves as a basis for academic or personnel decisions; interferes with performance or creates an intimidating, hostile, or offensive working or learning environment; or interferes with career development.

Courts have cited the following behavior as inappropriate within the workplace environment:

- Using terms such as "girls," "broads," or "skirts" in the workplace to refer to female employees;
- Telling sexual jokes in small groups of men—where women workers can overhear;

- Reading and commenting on magazines with sexually explicit articles and photographs; and
- Including men in activities that exclude women because they have nothing in common with men (Adams and Abarbanel 1992).

Obvious overt examples of sexual harassment may involve the promise of a promotion for sexual favors or less apparent situations in which appropriate disciplinary action is not taken in return for sexual favors.

WHAT IS THE NATURE AND PREVALENCE OF SEXUAL HARASSMENT ON CAMPUS?

Anyone on a campus—professors, advisors, teaching assistants, staff, administrators, maintenance workers, and students— can be sexually harassed. Harassment is not limited to the young and the attractive; often it happens to older adults. As with rape, vulnerability and naivete sometimes are key factors in the selection of victims (Hughes and Sandler 1986). As noted earlier, while both women and men can be harassed, women comprise the majority of victims. Although harassment of men by women exists as well as harassment by people of the same sex, these cases are relatively rare compared with the incidence of female harassment by males.

It was not until the early 1980s that sexual harassment was recognized as a problem of significant dimensions in higher education and incidents of harassment on campuses were documented by survey and published. Since that time, an enormous amount of attention has been focused on the issue, and the potential for institutional and individual liability has prompted colleges and universities to adopt policies to avert such problems. Further, increasing numbers of older women students, as well as a changing political climate in which women are more vocal and less inclined to tolerate discrimination, have brought pressure on colleges and universities to attend to issues of harassment. Moral and ethical concerns also have motivated institutions to eliminate sexual harassment.

However, because campuses have defined sexual harassment in different terms and collected information on the nature and prevalence of complaints employing varying methodologies, the comparability of statistics reported by these studies are questionable. In the future, institutions initiating such studies may wish to utilize the Sexual Experiences Questionnaire (Fitzgerald and Schulman 1985). This survey instrument, centering on student-professor experiences, has been the most frequent source of the incidence rates of student sexual harassment reported in the literature (Paludi and Barickman 1991c).

Following the 1986 Supreme Court decision in *Meritor,* educational institutions began to establish detailed policy statements to define and document the reality and effects of sexual harassment and to create careful procedures to address and prevent harassment. *Meritor* put institutions on notice that such complaints could no longer be ignored and that policies specifically prohibiting sexual harassment had to be put in place to protect students and employees from unwanted sexual advances and to discipline staff and students who make such advances, while also protecting the rights of the alleged perpetrators (Bayly 1990). Incidents of harassment among staff also were addressed by new policies. Once policies and procedures were in place and records were kept, it became possible to document the occurrences and to receive a much better picture of the problem.

The picture is not pretty. A recent issue of *The Chronicle of Higher Education* reports that from October to June of 1992, the EEOC received a total of 7,407 complaints of sexual harassment—524 more than in the previous 12 months (Leatherman 1992). The EEOC attributes this surge of complaints to reaction to the Anita Hill-Clarence Thomas hearings. Of the complaints filed, 1,834 have been resolved.

Officials have become more responsive and aggressive about hearing complaints, and their consciousness of the relations of the genders has become more acute. At large research and doctorate-granting institutions, more than 60 percent of the presidents surveyed said that sexual harassment was a problem, an indication of the level of awareness of the behavior (Boyer 1990).

Sexual Harassment of Students
During the last decade, surveys exploring the reported incidence of sexual harassment of students have been conducted at numerous institutions of higher learning (Williams, Lam, and Shively 1992). From 20 to 30 percent of undergraduate female college students reported experiencing some form of sexual harassment by at least one of their professors during their college years (Dzeich and Weiner 1984). Two percent of all female students, 125,000, experienced direct threats or bribes for sexual favors, and the incidence rate for women graduate students and faculty was even higher (Bailey and Richards 1985; Bond 1988).

Wilson and Kraus reported that 8.9 percent of the female undergraduates in their study had been touched, pinched, or patted to the point of personal discomfort (1983). In a study by Adams, Kotke, and Padgitt, 17 percent of women reported they had received verbal sexual advances, 13.6 percent had received sexual invitations, 6.4 percent had been subjected to physical advances, and 2 percent had received offers of direct sexual bribes (1983).

Bailey and Richards reported that of 246 women graduate students in their sample, 12.7 percent indicated that they had been sexually harassed, 21 percent had not enrolled in a course to avoid such behavior, 11.3 percent tried to report the behavior, 2.6 percent dropped a course because of it, and 15.9 percent indicated they had been directly assaulted (1985). Till claimed that graduate women in typically male-populated academic disciplines may be at disproportionate risk of being victimized (1980).

In a University of California at Berkeley study, more than 30 percent of undergraduate women students reported having received unwanted sexual attention from male faculty during their college years (Benson and Thompson 1982). Michigan State University researchers found that 25 percent of that institution's women students had been sexually harassed within the previous year (Maihoff and Forest 1983). McCormick et al. employed telephone interviews of female students enrolled at a small college and found that 14.8 percent had been victims of sexual harassment (1989).

In his study of sexual harassment of college students, Till identifies five hierarchical classes of sexual harassment: Type 1, gender harassment; Type 2, seductive behavior; Type 3, sexual bribery; Type 4, sexual coercion; and Type 5, sexual imposition or assault (1980). This classification system may serve as an important model for institutions in examining and responding to sexual harassment on their campuses.

The results of these institutional studies affirm that sexual harassment is a problem for significant proportions of female students. The best means by which a university can remedy the growing problem and shield itself from potential liability is to educate all students, staff, and faculty and to develop and enforce a strong sexual harassment policy (Connolly and Marshall 1989).

Peer Sexual Harassment

Peer harassment describes the sexual harassment of women by their male colleagues—women students by male students; women faculty by male faculty; gay and lesbian students by other students (Paludi and Barickman 1991b). Sexual harassment among peers has been responsible for some of the most unfortunate incidents on campuses. When definitions of harassment include sexist remarks and other forms of gender harassment, the incidence rate among undergraduate females exceeds 75 percent (Adams, Kotke, and Padgitt 1983; Lott, Reilly, and Howard 1982).

In 1986, Cornell University surveyed its women students and found that 78 percent of those responding had experienced one or more forms of peer harassment, including sexist comments and unwelcome attention. Thirty-seven percent of the undergraduate women reported being subjected to more serious forms of unwanted sexual attention. While most of these experiences involved individual men, a substantial percentage involved groups of men who committed the most serious forms of harassment in fraternity houses, stadiums, and at parties. Massachusetts Institute of Technology reported that 92 percent of its women students were sexually harassed by peers, and the University of Rhode Island reported 70 percent experienced such behavior (Hughes and Sandler 1986).

In an even more severe manifestation of the problem, Rhodes has estimated that one in eight women nationally is raped by a friend or acquaintance sometime during her college career (1992). Date rape is a problem of alarming proportions—80 percent of which occur on Saturday nights after alcohol has been used (Rhodes 1992).

In their comprehensive discussion of peer harassment, Hughes and Sandler further assert, "A picture is emerging of too many young men on campus engaging in behaviors that can best be described as emotional and psychological harassment. Such behaviors, which are often invasive and disrespectful, can poison the college experience for women. Although some of these behaviors may at first glance appear to be individual, unrelated acts, they are instead part of a pattern representing widespread group behavior" (1986, pp. 1-2). The authors' recommendations for addressing peer harassment are consistent with the recommendations for dealing with the broader dimensions of sexual harassment discussed in this report.

Sexual Harassment of Non-Faculty Employees
Few studies focus on the harassment of non-faculty employees in the college and university system. However, there is no reason to assume that the harassment of college staff is any less than the 50 percent rate reported for employees of various other public and private institutions (Fitzgerald et al. 1988). Goodwin found in her study of university employees that 39 percent of the women and 19 percent of the men indi-

cated they had experienced some form of sexual harassment (1989). Both the male and the female employees indicated that male co-workers were most often the perpetrators. Dziech notes that in the workplace victims avoid private and public contacts with harassers and frequently are absent from work, often impairing their job performance, limiting advancement, and resulting in lower wages or other sanctions (1991).

Fear of Filing a Complaint

One of the most serious issues for institutions to consider is that of fear on the part of the victim of complaining formally.

Rowe described eight characteristics that defined the feelings of 95 percent of the people who complained to her office of harassment:

- A fear of retaliation and reprisal;
- A fear of the loss of privacy;
- A feeling of discomfort because of a lack of conclusive proof of the alleged event;
- A sense of limited skills;
- A feeling of lack of loyalty;
- A sense that it is absolutely pointless to complain;
- A dislike of losing control over the complaint; and
- A desire for the harassment to stop (1987).

College students cut classes, change majors, relinquish careers, and drop out of school to avoid harassers.

The remaining 5 percent were more aggressive. They wanted to see the problem investigated and settled fairly and promptly through an advocate.

Dziech contends that one of the greatest difficulties that victims face is their own "avoidance response" (1991). Females generally have been socialized to avoid confrontation; therefore, most refuse to confront harassers or protest or file grievances. Many victims also cope by trying to avoid the perpetrators. College students cut classes, change majors, relinquish careers, and drop out of school to avoid harassers.

One proposal to counter the reluctance to report harassing behavior has been suggested by Sundt (1993). She writes,

. . . we need to do a better job of empowering victims of harassment to tell their story. Ironically, policies prohibiting all sexual relationships reinforce victimization because they imply that victims can neither protect themselves from being

exploited nor distinguish between healthy and coercive rela-
tionships. Similarly, procedures that require action even
when the victim is unwilling to proceed may make the insti-
tution feel avenged but leave the victim once again pow-
erless and discourage other victims from reporting
(pp. 333-34).

Clearly, colleges and universities are obligated to create an
environment in which women are encouraged to develop
to their fullest potential and exercise their rights to have their
grievances redressed. Proactive programs to educate and
inform members of the academic community of their rights
and responsibilities in human relationships seem imperative.

Gender Differences in Attitudes Toward Sexual Harassment

Fuehrer and Schilling suggested that there is a difference of
opinion between men and women about what a common
set of behaviors means (1988). Hacker states that often the
male harasser does not realize that his actions or comments
are offensive, since the female usually does not openly object
(1991). When the man is in a position of power, such as
employer or teacher, the woman may feel coerced or forced
to submit. In addition, many men believe a woman's "no"
is really "yes," and therefore do not accept her refusal
(Hughes and Sandler 1986).

Fitzgerald and Weitzman reported that sexual harassers
often have a reputation for harassment, and most women
report that the person who has harassed them also has
approached other women (1988). Pryor related that the likelihood of sexual harassment is related to gender-role stereo-
typing and is negatively related to feminist attitudes and to
that component of empathy pertaining to the ability to take
the viewpoint of the other (1987).

In a 1986 unpublished survey commissioned by *Time* mag-
azine, a majority of both men and women held similar views
relative to what constitutes harassment: repeated sexual
remarks to a co-worker of the opposite sex, pressure invitations for dinner on a regular basis, and frequently placing an
arm around a co-worker's shoulders. But other studies have
not shown this male/female consensus (Clark 1991).

Citing evidence that suggests that female and male college
students are reporting more similar experiences of sexual

harassment, Dietz-Uhler and Murrell write that their research
". . . showed that although men and women differed some-
what in their attitudes toward sexual harassment, there were
no sex differences in their judgment of specific sexual harassment behaviors" (1992, p. 543). The authors further conclude
that (1) males tended to be more tolerant in their global attitudes toward sexual harassment; (2) that the more that individuals accepted the stereotypical roles of males and females,
the more tolerant they tended to be in terms of the attitudes
toward sexual harassment; and (3) that when men endorse
the stereotypical roles of men and women, they are less likely
to take seriously the issues of sexual harassment.

In view of these inconsistent conclusions, it seems important for institutions of higher education to provide opportunities for males and females to engage in a dialogue about
these differences in perception. One of the values in the educational and communication aspects of sexual harassment
policies is the resulting conversations that might occur. An
open discussion regarding what is acceptable and what is
intolerable must occur to bring expectations and behaviors
more closely in line.

Why Does Sexual Harassment Occur?
Numerous reasons have been suggested for the persistence
of sexual harassment. The most common explanation is
derived from the sociocultural model that states that sexual
harassment reflects the larger society's differential distribution
of power and status between the sexes and that men harass
to maintain their dominance in economic and social relationships (Whitmore 1983). The organizational model posited
by Dziech and Weiner argues that sexual harassment is a by-
product of an organization's climate, hierarchy, and authority
relations including diffused institutional authority, as well as
a lack of accountability and mutual respect for professional
autonomy (1984).

Tangri, Burt, and Johnson looked at sexual harassment from
a cultural standpoint, taking into account the motivation, facil-
itation, and power differentials between males and females
(1982). In their review of the available literature, they developed three models: (1) the natural or biological model, (2)
the organizational model, and (3) the sociocultural model.

The natural model states that harassment stems from naturally occurring sexual attraction between people. There are two subtypes of this model; one subtype explains the male's stronger sex drive with no intent to harass, and the second subtype postulates that either sex can be attracted to the other and may pursue that person with positive motives. This model states that there is no intention to discriminate against women or to reduce their chances of success in their vocation.

The organizational model shows that sexual harassment is the result of an organization's vertical hierarchy, authority structure, and climate. The proportion of men and women within the organization can help or hinder displays of sexual harassment, depending on the personalities within a work unit and the overall social context. Some vocations, such as those where appearance is important, can overtly foster sexual harassment. Sexual harassment is negative in this model, since vocational mobility, visibility, and availability of grievance procedures and job alternatives can be reduced.

The sociocultural model looks at the males' possession of greater power and status over women in society. Male dominance is perceived as necessary within the economic and political climate, and traditional social beliefs reinforce this dominance. There may or may not be conscious collaboration among men to keep the status quo in this model. Men are rewarded for domineering and aggressive behavior, while the self-esteem and worth of women is derived from the judgments of others. Females have been socialized to accept the subordinate position and to accept male attention as flattery.

In both the organizational model and the sociocultural model, sexual harassment has a negative connotation. The organizational model would be most supportive of women seeking redress from such harassment, while in the sociocultural model women would not be expected to file such complaints.

Gutek and Morasch proposed a theory that appears to combine aspects of the theories of Tangri, Burt, and Johnson which they called "sex-role spillover" (1982). In this theory, women are expected to be sex objects or to demonstrate their sexuality through their appearance and behavior in all aspects of their lives. In male-dominated professional fields, the traditional role of women as subordinate to men is facilitated by the dearth of women in power within the organizations. In traditionally female-dominated professions, the professional role and the gender role are intertwined. Men want to react to women at work as they do toward women in their personal lives, and women accommodate this request. In all of these respects, conditioned sex roles are "spilled over" and reinforced in the occupational setting.

The sexual assault of women and its resulting physical and psychological damage has spurred the development of unified models of the bases of sexual aggression. Many clinical researchers have tried to ascertain the causes of sexual aggression in order to develop intervention and treatment programs, define the problems and characteristics of offenders, and advise the courts on decisions for convicted offenders. The available data show that male sexual aggressors are heterogeneous and present no single cause of sexually aggressive behavior (Hall, Hirschman, and Beutler 1991).

The study of such models and their applicability to higher education holds promise on two fronts. One is a greater eventual understanding of the behavior of the perpetrator and the motivation behind her or his harassment. The second is perhaps more likely to yield immediate benefit, and it results from the illumination that can come from the study itself. As the problem of harassment is acknowledged, researched, and discussed on campus, the nature of the problem will change. As was mentioned earlier, the resulting dialogue, it is hoped, will bring about a greater understanding between people regarding what is acceptable behavior and what is not.

Sexual Harassment Effects on the Victim

Paludi and Barickman suggest that institutions of higher education are not equipped to accommodate sexual harassment issues; thus, reports of such behaviors are trivialized as "personal relation issues outside the control of the institution and unrelated to its own powers and prerogatives" (1991b, p. 150).

Due to this inability to effectively handle sexual harassment reports and the ensuing investigations, colleges and universities, in effect, isolate and "hold up for example" (Koss 1990) victims of sexual harassment. Riger further argues that the secrecy involved in reporting sexual harassment stigmatizes the victim's experience (1991). Such stigmatization reinforces the victim's already perceived position of powerlessness. Brown also points out the innate control given to institutions based on a white, male, middle-class perspective that denies equal access for women to fair treatment and makes sexual harassment "annoying" instead of "traumatic" (1991).

Victims' trauma response to sexual harassment has been likened to the trauma response to rape (Koss 1990; Paludi and Barickman 1991a; Quina 1990; Sandler 1990). Such responses include physiological, psychological, and sociological reactions to internal and external stressors related to the sexual assault—in this case, sexual harassment.

Women who have experienced sexual harassment and then discussed their experiences report such physiological responses as headaches, bruxism, muscular tension and spasms, gastrointestinal disturbances, and generalized fatigue (Bradway 1992; Crull 1982; Gutek 1981; Koss 1990; Project on the Status of Women and Education 1978; Paludi and Barickman 1991a).

Psychological impact also can be seen in victims' reports of feelings of loss of control, helplessness, and decreased motivation. Depression and intrusion of thoughts related to the sexual harassment that affect ability to maintain cognitive focus and also impair sleep processes are further psychological effects of sexual harassment (Bradway 1992; Hotelling 1991; Koss 1990; Project on the Status of Women and Education 1978).

Victims of sexual harassment also may experience economic crises (Hamilton et al. 1987) as a result of being denied a position or promotion (Howard 1991), leaving a position for fear of further redress or being fired (Koss 1990), and/or loss of references from the institution or department where the harassment occurred (Hamilton et al. 1987). The economic impact deepens when victims already experiencing loss of wages or loss of promotion then must secure legal counsel (Riger 1991) and psychological assistance (Koss 1990; Rabinowitz 1990; Sandler 1990) to cope with the institution's grievance system.

Such psychological and sociological trauma clearly interferes with one's functioning in an educational setting, whether as a student, faculty member, or in a staff or support capacity. Colleges and universities have an obligation to provide support and backing for students and employees both during the harassment procedures and following their resolution, in the same way that colleges and universities are required by law to provide support and backing in cases of assault or rape.

Rehabilitation for the Victim

The victim's opportunities for redress against the offender and opportunities for rehabilitation within the institution depend in large part on the specific institution's policies and procedures. D'Ercole (1988) and Brown (1991) suggest that the first change institutions must make in providing fair opportunity for redress for victims is to acknowledge a feminist viewpoint and sensitize the community to the predominantly male-oriented political and social structures underlying sexual harassment. The Alliance Against Sexual Coercion (1980) and others (Howard 1991; Paludi and Barickman 1991b) add that victims need to be assured of a confidential, impartial, and viable grievance procedure not only as an opportunity for redress but also as part of the victims' healing process.

Assistance in emotional and physical healing for victims of sexual harassment is imperative. Fitzgerald et al. point out that ". . . sexual harassment constitutes one of the most damaging barriers to women's career success and satisfaction" (1988, p. 163). Rabinowitz adds to that cognitive, behavioral, emotional, and physical damage (1990). Koss further says that injury from sexual harassment is long-term due to the unpredictable and long-lasting nature of the trauma and damage (1990).

Paludi and Barickman suggest that part of the rehabilitation program for victims should be an institutional effort to establish a confidential and equitable protocol for management of sexual harassment complaints (1991b). Riger provides more in-depth guidelines for such protocols, pointing out that colleges and universities often mistakenly assume that a woman filing a complaint has equal power to the male who is the accused (1991). Riger calls for institution-appointed and trained advocates to assist women in the rehabilitation and legal/grievance procedures following sexual assault.

Further suggestions for assisting sexual harassment victims in the healing process include that the institution should: (1) provide trained counselors to work with victims (D'Ercole 1988; Sandler 1990; Shullman 1989; Lundberg-Love 1989); (2) offer workshops or group counseling for victims in areas of self-efficacy, assertiveness, stress management, and problem solving for victims (Rabinowitz 1990); and (3) develop workshops to educate people who work with the victims and offenders about sexual harassment and its effects (Howard 1991; Paludi and Barickman 1991b). Sandler (1990) and the Project for the Status on Women and Education (1978) further suggest that institutions establish a 24-hour crisis hotline for victims of sexual harassment to call for information and support.

Rabinowitz (1990) and Koss (1990) say that the most important assistance for sexual harassment victims is validation of the victims' feelings and experiences. Such validation can come in individual counseling, group work, grievance processes, and from any individuals who can provide support to the victim. Specialists using cognitive readjustment techniques can provide rehabilitation assistance for victims (Janoff-Bulman and Frieze 1983; Taylor 1983) by helping the victim express anger and search for meaning of the experience (Koss 1990); work through denial, avoidance, and deceit coping methods (Rabinowitz 1990); resolve issues of confusion/self-blame, fear/anxiety, depression/anger, and disillusionment (Salisbury et al. 1986); and overcome what may be heightened symptoms in cases where the victim does not file a complaint of the harassment (Livingston 1982).

As Koss (1990) and Sandler (1990) have noted, colleges and universities must formulate policies and procedures to handle sexual assault grievances; however, in such systematic reasoning, most do not address programs to assist the victim with traumatization. While Koss (1990) and others (D'Ercole 1988; Brown 1991) call for counseling for victims of sexual harassment within the college or university, they offer only suggestions for programs, not outlines for conducting such rehabilitation.

Calhoun and Atkeson are among the many psychosocial practitioners who address sexual assault rehabilitation through crisis intervention counseling (1991). As Koss (1990), Paludi and Barickman (1991a), Quina (1990), and Sandler (1990) have pointed out, sexual harassment is a form of sexual assault and may result in cognitive and behavioral trauma responses similar to those of rape. While crisis intervention has not been evaluated empirically for its effect on post-assault readjustment, many practitioners and theorists (e.g., Burgess and Holmstrom 1979; Kilpatrick and Veronen 1983; Kilpatrick, Veronen, and Resick 1982) support its use. As with sexual assault, crisis intervention therapy is a model that could be instituted at colleges and universities to work with sexual harassment victims.

Crisis intervention rehabilitation can start with the establishment of a 24-hour crisis hotline (Project on the Status of Women and Education 1978; Sandler 1990). Such a hotline would be staffed by professionals or paraprofessionals and could offer emotional stabilization and information dissemination.

On a larger scale, colleges and universities should provide counselors who are trained to address the following issues with sexual harassment victims:

- Encourage victims to express emotions and validate those feelings;
- Provide factual information regarding the options for redress and rehabilitation;
- Assist victims in identifying future needs for coping skills;
- Assist victims in adjusting role responsibilities to reduce stress;
- Assist victims in identifying a network for social support and help decide how to mobilize that network; and
- Help victims make a follow-up plan so that assistance is available whenever it is needed (Calhoun and Atkeson 1991).

Koss adds to the crisis intervention model that victims of sexual harassment specifically need to address feelings of anger, injustice, and hopelessness (1990). She further suggests that counselors working with sexual harassment victims help them search for meaning in the harassment situation, for it is through cognitive understanding that behavioral rehabilitation can begin.

At the minimum, higher education institutions should offer crisis intervention assistance for victims. Beyond such intervention, colleges and universities should consider integrating services available through counseling on campus and women's resource centers (either on campus or in the community) for long-term rehabilitation assistance (Sandler 1990). The Campus Sexual Assault Victims' Bill of Rights addressed earlier offers legal impetus for victims' rehabilitation by requiring the provision of counseling and psychiatric assistance. Coupled with institutions' concern for the well-being and continued development of all students and employees, it puts the welfare and restitution of the victim in a central place.

Consensual Amorous Relationships

One of the most perplexing issues facing college and university policy makers is the dilemma of consensual sexual relations between faculty and students or supervisors and subordinates. On the one hand, there is the issue of trust and respect of faculty members and university supervisors in positions of responsibility over students and other members of the university community. As suggested by Zalk, Dederich, and Paludi, "The bottom line is power. The faculty member has it and the student does not" (1991, p. 101). The assertion is that within the context of such a power imbalance that an amorous relationship, even with the consent of both parties, is damaging to the educational process and should be prohibited.

A second view holds that individual rights to privacy, freedom of association, and the civil right to engage in intimate relationships without governmental interference militate against institutional policies that seek to prohibit consensual amorous relationships between students and faculty. Keller provides a thorough discussion of the constitutional and case laws that impact on the issue (1988). She asserts, "Outside the instructional context, the presumption that an intimate faculty-student relationship results from coercion cannot be justified" (p. 40). She continues,

> *A bright-line test can thus be formulated for public universities defining the area of permissible state intrusion into constitutionally protected private relationships: the university may proscribe the formation of intimate faculty-student relationships within the instructional context, namely, when the faculty member academically supervises the student. Intimate consensual relationships falling outside the instructional context are constitutionally protected from university interference* (p. 41).

In response to this issue, a number of colleges and universities have implemented policies that either criticize or prohibit consensual relationships between faculty and students (National Association for Women in Education 1992). The University of Iowa, in establishing the context for its policy dealing with consensual relations, declares that amorous relationships between faculty members and students are wrong when the faculty member has professional responsibility for the student (1991). In such cases—even with voluntary consent by the student—such a relationship is suspect, given the fundamentally asymmetric nature of the relationship. The university's policy proceeds to prohibit amorous relations between a faculty member and a student enrolled in the professor's course or under his or her academic supervision. Relationships outside the instructional context, while not directly prohibited, are strongly discouraged, and the faculty member in such situations is held accountable to explicit ethical obligations.

"The bottom line is power. The faculty member has it and the student does not."

Vermont State College defines unethical conduct by a faculty member as encompassing amorous and sexual relationships between a student and faculty member and asserts such relations to be entirely inappropriate (1991). The college's policy suggests that initially consensual relationships may not protect the institution from subsequent charges of sexual harassment if the relationship turns sour.

The board of trustees of Antioch College has adopted a policy for its Yellow Springs, Ohio, campus that declares that sexual relations between faculty and students are unacceptable and constitute professional misconduct (Mulhauser 1992). In contrast to this position, Antioch campuses in California, Washington, and New Hampshire (where the average student age is in the forties) hesitated to adopt the policy. Instead, students and faculty asserted that, in an atmosphere in which trusted adults are encouraged to behave reasonably, written policies were not necessary. They suggested that consensual sexual relations should not be regarded differently from other consensual relationships in which a power imbalance exists— such as in business or psychotherapeutic relationships.

The University of Virginia recently drew national attention when considering a controversial plan initiated by a University Advisory Committee on Women's Issues that would ban sexual relationships between professors and undergraduates (Mooney 1993). In addition, the proposal would forbid professors to make overtures to or have sexual relationships with graduate students who are in the courses of, under the supervision of, or enrolled in programs in the same department as the professor.

George Rutherglen, a law professor at the university, argues that the proposal's general prohibition against any relationships between faculty and undergraduates would not violate privacy rights of faculty members and students (personal communication 1993). He believes that such a prohibition could be justified for at least three reasons:

First, affairs between faculty and students threaten the integrity of the university as an educational institution. Such relationships interfere with the disinterested pursuit of knowledge, compromise the impartiality of the faculty member in teaching and evaluating other students, and often cause emotional problems for the students who are parties to the relationship. Affairs with students also are likely to violate a faculty member's professional duty, recognized by the American Association of University Professors (AAUP) Statement of Professional Ethics, to avoid "any exploitation of students for his private advantage." Although some cases may not pose these problems, a university may address general problems with general rules.

Second, affairs between faculty and students expose the university to liability for sexual harassment under Title IX of the Education Amendments of 1972, which prohibits sex-based discrimination by recipients of federal funds. Sexual harassment may arise from a consensual sexual relationship at any point when sexual advances become unwelcome.

As the Supreme Court has made clear in *Meritor,* consent is no defense to a claim of sexual harassment. Whether affairs between faculty and students result in sexual harassment inevitably depends on the facts of each case, which are likely to be disputed if the affair ends acrimoniously. For this reason, a recipient of federal funds, such as the University of Virginia, might well take precautions to avoid liability by prohibiting all sexual relations between faculty and students. Even apart from exposure to liability, of course, the university also can take steps to minimize the risk of sexual harassment.

Third, the university may act to prevent the public outcry that inevitably would follow upon any publicized incident of sexual harassment or sexual relations between faculty and students. A public university must be especially concerned about its public image, which would likely suffer from any impression that it condoned sexual relations between faculty and students.

The 1984 AAUP policy statement dealing with sexual harassment reiterates the ethical responsibilities of faculty not to exploit students for any personal advantage, cites sexual harassment as unprofessional conduct, and strongly suggests that institutions should not condone abuses by faculty members of the academic freedom of others with respect to sexual harassment (1990a, pp. 113-14). In a recent revision of the 1984 report, the AAUP suggests language for institutional policies dealing with sexual harassment (1990b). A footnote to this AAUP proposal admonishes, "Faculty members and staff are cautioned against entering romantic or sexual relationships with their students; so, too, is a supervisor cautioned against entering such relationships with an employee. Faculty and staff should be cautious in assuming professional responsibilities for those with whom they have an existing romantic relationship" (AAUP 1990b, p. 42).

In a similar theme, the National Education Association (NEA) has declared sexual relations between a faculty member and a currently supervised student to be unprofessional. The association incorporated a resolution into NEA policy in 1989, which states:

> *The National Education Association recognizes that in institutions of higher education, adult students and educators may establish personal relationships. However, such relationships should be voluntary and not be used to coerce or influence others for personal advantage. Thus, the Association believes that sexual relationships between a faculty member and a student currently enrolled in the faculty member's course, or under the supervision or direction of the faculty member, are unprofessional. The Association urges its affiliates in institutions of higher education to establish strong policies declaring such relationships unprofessional* (Resolution I-20 1989, NEA 1992).

Wagner (1990) and Paludi (1990) report concerns on several campuses about whether there exists "consensual" sex between faculty and students or between those of unequal status. The issue of power threatens any sexual relationship when one has it and the other does not. Further, this type of relationship may be viewed by other students or employees as engendering preferential treatment or as fostering prejudicial evaluation, giving an unfair advantage to one student or employee over another (Mulhauser 1992).

Issues of trust, authority, privacy, and power make the area of consensual relationships complex and difficult. Most policies advise against such relationships where one party has responsibility for personnel or academic decisions regarding the other party. A major component of the problem is the sometimes transitory nature of human relationships and the potential for amorous liaisons to turn sour, resulting in subsequent charges of sexual harassment. Few institutions, however, relish the idea of monitoring such relationships, and an appeal to professionalism and ethical conduct on the part of faculty and staff along with educational programs for students may be the most effective preventive tools.

EFFECTIVE POLICY AND PRACTICE FOR
THE ELIMINATION OF SEXUAL HARASSMENT

Perhaps the greatest mistake an institution of higher learning can make is not having in place, *prior* to receiving a sexual harassment complaint, well-developed policies and procedures for handling the situation. The American Council on Education (ACE) statement stresses the importance of developing a campus program on sexual harassment:

> *The educational mission of a college or university is to foster an open learning and working environment. The ethical obligation to provide an environment that is free from sexual harassment and from fear that it may occur is implicit. The entire collegiate community suffers when sexual harassment is allowed to pervade the academic atmosphere through neglect, the lack of a policy prohibiting it, or the lack of educational programs designed to clarify appropriate professional behavior on campus and to promote understanding of what constitutes sexual harassment. Each institution has the obligation, for moral as well as legal reasons, to develop policies, procedures, and programs that protect students and employees from sexual harassment and to establish an environment in which such unacceptable behavior will not be tolerated* (1986, 1993, p. 2).

As was shown in the Meritor case, the existence of a broad anti-discrimination policy probably will not be adequate, and institutions are better served by specifically addressing sexual harassment. Taking preventive steps can help shield an institution from potential legal liability as well as address legitimate constituent concerns. Further, such an approach utilizes the educational process—its *raison d'etre*—to accomplish its goals.

Wagner asserts that "to be credible, policies must have three goals—preventing harassment, remedying situations which occur, and dealing with perpetrators. . . . Institutional definitions of sexual harassment and approaches for dealing with it that are informed by the experiences of women and sensitive to the complexities of the issue will be most effective" (1990). Following this admonition not only protects the institution from claims of sexism in the actual process of policy formulation but uses the process to promote understanding among the policy makers.

While each institution should design a unique policy based on local and situational needs, ACE and others have suggested five elements that constitute good policy and practices to prevent or handle sexual harassment on campus:

1. A definition of sexual harassment.
2. A strong policy statement indicating intolerance of sexual harassment.
3. Effective communication with those involved or with those subject to the provisions.
4. Education of everyone.
5. An accessible grievance procedure (Dozier 1990; Wagner 1990).

Because this seems to be the most often used list of requirements for a sexual harassment policy, each element is defined separately below and in more detail.

A Basic Definition of Sexual Harassment

As indicated earlier, arriving at a definition of sexual harassment is not an easy task. Guidelines suggested by ACE, AAUP, EEOC, and other organizations may be used to ensure that all possibilities have been included that are appropriate for a given institution. Care should be taken to avoid a reductionistic definition that may preclude recognition of more elusive or cumulative forms of harassment.

The Yale University School of Medicine uses the following definition in its sexual harassment policy:

> *Sexual harassment is antithetical to academic values and to a work environment free from the fact or appearance of coercion, and it is a violation of University policy. Sexual harassment consists of nonconsensual sexual advances, requests for sexual favors, or other verbal or physical conduct of a sexual nature on or off campus, when: (1) submission to such conduct is made either explicitly or implicitly a condition of an individual's employment or academic standing; or (2) submission to or rejection of such conduct is used as the basis for employment decisions or for academic evaluation, grades, or advancement; or (3) such conduct has the purpose or effect of unreasonably interfering with an individual's work environment. Sexual harassment may be found in a single episode, as well as in persistent behavior (1986).*

The Georgia Institute of Technology definition contrasts
sexual harassment with voluntary sexual relations as follows
in its materials:

*Sexual harassment differs from voluntary sexual relations
in that sexual harassment involves unwanted sexual attention, threat, or coercion.*

*Sexual harassment is defined as unwelcome sexual
advances, requests for sexual favors, or physical contact
of a sexual nature. Such behavior constitutes sexual harassment when:*

*Acceptance or rejection becomes a condition of your
employment or academic standing.*

*Acceptance or rejection serves as a basis for academic
or personnel decisions which concern you.*

*Such conduct interferes with your performance or creates
an intimidating, hostile or offensive working or learning
environment* (1988).

The University of South Carolina defines sexual harassment
in this way:

It is illegal!
*Sexual harassment is a form of sex discrimination which
is prohibited under Federal and State laws:*
Title VII of the Civil Rights Act of 1964
Title IX of the Education Amendments of 1972
The South Carolina Human Affairs Law
It comes in many forms . . .
*Sexual harassment can be directed at a person of the
same or opposite sex.*
*Behaviors that are considered as sexual harassment
include:*
unwelcome sexual advances,
requests for sexual favors,
*language, graphic material, or physical conduct com-
monly understood to be of a sexual nature,*
demeaning sexist remarks,
other verbal or physical conduct of a sexual nature
(1990).

Each of these definitions is congruent with the definition of
sexual harassment presented earlier in this report. They

acknowledge the role of the *victim's* perception of the harassing behavior, they include both *quid pro quo* harassment and hostile environment harassment, and they define sexual harassment sufficiently broadly to avoid narrow technical interpretations. They also meet Mulhauser's criteria for specificity and clarity (1992), and the language is free of bias.

A Strong Policy Statement Necessary

After defining sexual harassment, the institution is obligated to make a strong statement that sexual harassment will not be tolerated. Some statements are short and concise, such as that of Tennessee's Union University:

Union [University] is committed to providing its faculty, staff, and students with an environment free from explicit and implicit coercive sexual behavior used to control, influence, or affect the well-being of any member of the College community. Sexual harassment of any person is inappropriate and unacceptable, and is grounds for disciplinary action, including termination of employment. Faculty are asked to be especially sensitive to allegations of sexual harassment resulting from private, one-on-one associations with students both on-campus and off-campus (1992).

Other statements are broader in nature, such as that of St. Cloud State University in Minnesota:

The Minnesota State University System is committed to ensuring an educational and employment environment free of sexual harassment, sexual violence/assault, harassment based on gender, sexual orientation/affectional preference, racial and disability intolerance. Such behaviors have no place in the University or work environment where students, faculty, and staff are expected to learn and develop to their full potential. Harassing and violent behaviors which impede that potential are unacceptable within this System (1992).

Or that of Carleton College, also in Minnesota:

When sexual harassment occurs at Carleton College, the standards of the community are violated. Sexual harassment of any student, faculty member, or employee by any

other student, faculty member, or employee is prohibited
and will not be tolerated.

Retaliation against a person who reports, complains
about, or participates in the investigation of sexual harass-
ment is also intolerable and prohibited.

Students, faculty, and staff are reminded that apparently
consensual sexual relationships, particularly those between
individuals of unequal status, may be or may quickly
become violative of this policy. The College particularly
abhors the abuse potentially inherent in sexual relationships
between faculty members and their students (1990).

These statements are all unequivocal in declaring sexual
harassment unacceptable. While they include all members
of the college community, they highlight the relationships
of faculty and students. The Carleton statement specifically
prohibits retaliation and protects those involved in the complaint and investigation. This statement also addresses the
issue of consensual sexual relationships, a topic that is especially important from the standpoint of educating students.

The University of Iowa, Harvard University, Hampshire College, University of Minnesota, and the University of Pennsylvania also have developed policy statements about consensual
relationships (Association of American Colleges). The Union
University caution regarding one-on-one relationships
between faculty and students, while aimed specifically at faculty in this instance, serves to alert students to the potential
danger involved as well.

Effective Communication
A method of informing faculty, staff, and students of policies
is necessary if compliance is to be achieved. Faculty, staff, and
student handbooks should contain the policy and procedures
concerning sexual harassment. It may be necessary to call
attention to these statements and to reiterate the information
from time to time since this type of policy is one that, it is
hoped, will not be used often. The person who has been
harassed or the person to whom harassment has been con-
fided may not remember that such a policy exists or where
it may be found. For this reason, the policy should be printed
in a number of places—all of which are accessible to anyone
concerned—thus decreasing the chances that an incident may
be blown out of proportion before the accused has had the

opportunity to respond. It is important that each new student and each new employee be advised of the policy. Posters, memos, fliers, and radio announcements are all available communication devices.

One of the most important means of communicating the policy is through a strong education program. Indeed, the two elements are complementary, and it may be argued that communication has not taken place unless there is the understanding and shared meaning that comes through education.

An Accessible Grievance Procedure

Rowe warns that "an institution that designs its harassment procedures for itself rather than its complainants will not do as well as an institution that decides to improve its productivity by designing its services to fit its particular kind of consumer" (1987). ACE, in its recently revised guidelines, states, "A grievance procedure should be developed that encourages the reporting of incidents of sexual harassment, that allows first for informal resolution and then, if the process fails, for formal resolution. The procedure should establish several alternate individuals with whom the claim may be raised in order to enable the employee to circumvent the accused harasser and to encourage victims to come forward" (1993, p. 2).

In designing a grievance procedure for handling harassment charges, it may help institutions to look at the grievance procedures—grade challenges, other charges against faculty, discrimination cases, and even promotion disagreements, for example—that are already in place for handling other types of situations. Although some of the current procedures might be the same as those needed for dealing with sexual harassment, it may be preferable that a completely separate procedure should be devised because of the sensitive and confidential nature of complaints. Even when separate procedures are instituted, however, it is helpful if there is some degree of congruence and parallel structure in the administrative protocols.

Wagner counsels that "[g]rievance mechanisms must be designed to encourage individuals to come forward, must protect complainants against retaliation, and should be flexible enough to allow both informal and formal resolutions" (1990). Time limits for reporting may be specified but should not be unnecessarily short, since it may take some time for a victim to find the courage to make a complaint. Provisions should be made for a student to file a complaint at the end of a semester or even after graduation. The procedure should specify a number of people who could be contacted with the complaint. These people should be accessible, open, and trained to handle the sensitive character of the problem.

Informal channels may include simply talking to a counselor or committee member, since most individuals would prefer to resolve the situations through in-house channels. They usually just want the harassment to stop, and accomplishing that as quickly and as confidentially as possible is the prime motive of most complainants (Dzeich and Weiner 1984).

Sandler has developed an outline for a three-part letter to be sent to the harasser by the individual being harassed (1983). Part I tells the facts about the situation, without evaluation. It states times, dates, and places of the incident(s) in as much detail as possible. Part II describes how the writer feels about the incident(s) described in the first part, such as, "I am embarrassed to come to your class now." Part III states what the writer wants to happen next, such as, "I do not want you ever to touch me again." The writer should keep a copy of the letter and either deliver it personally in the presence of a witness or send it by registered mail. Sandler says that often this is all that is needed to stop the behavior. If the accused had offended the complainant in ignorance, this would give her or him the opportunity to apologize and to rectify the behavior.

Helly reports that Hunter College of the City University of New York has effectively employed a Sexual Harassment Panel to informally adjudicate complaints of sexual harassment (1987). The panel, with membership representative of the campus community, seeks to achieve resolution of complaints through informal discussion that leads to correcting or remedying the injury and the prevention of further harassment.

Weddle advocates that institutions adopt the procedure of structured negotiation in lieu of formal adjudication (1992). She defines structured negotiation as ". . . a process of facilitated educational dialogue between directly aggrieved and accused students where the goal of the process is to reach mutually acceptable outcomes as to undertakings and actions on the part of one or both parties in lieu of formal adjudication of guilt" (p. 291). Utilization of this resolution alter-

Concern for the rights of the claimant and of the accused should be shown in the impartiality of the proceedings.

native is asserted to have several advantages in sexual misconduct cases including full student empowerment, timely resolution, privacy and confidentiality, and a developmental or educational nature.

Other informal ways of dealing with a charge include informing the supervisor of the problem without specifying those involved and asking that a letter be sent to all department members reminding them of the policy. Reiterating the policy in a faculty meeting or showing a video or conducting a workshop dealing with harassment sometimes helps. Whatever informal resolution procedure an institution may utilize, it is important that documentation of the complaint resolution be maintained. This institutional sign-off is essential in the event the harassing behavior reappears.

If the problem is not solved in informal ways, a procedure should be designated to provide for formal charges to be made, still keeping the matter as confidential as possible. Care should be taken to ensure that the accused has the opportunity to respond to the charge before serious, sometimes permanent, damage to her or his reputation is done. The procedure should provide for a prompt investigation and a hearing before a panel or committee of faculty, staff, and students. It should be made clear that retaliation against the claimant, witnesses, and investigators will not be tolerated (Wagner 1990).

Concern for the rights of the claimant and of the accused should be shown in the impartiality of the proceedings. When a decision has been reached and disposition has been made, all parties should be advised of the action and penalties imposed, if any. Howard suggests that the goal of the proceedings should be "to take corrective action, . . . prevent recurrence, . . . and maintain the integrity of the academic community and environment" (cited in Wagner 1990). Employee assistance programs, women's centers, and student services can provide professional counseling for either or both parties.

The claimant still may not be satisfied with the decision, in which case he or she might file a civil lawsuit or criminal charges if appropriate or seek the intervention of an advocacy group, such as the EEOC, affirmative action groups, the NEA, or the AAUP. Mulhauser emphasizes that the policy should make clear that the justice system is an option, as is the use of the institution's procedures, and that both avenues, or neither, may be pursued (1992).

Education

As indicated earlier, communication of the policy goes hand in hand with education. A plan for making the entire college community aware of sexual harassment, its implications, and procedures for its handling is mandatory to achieve effective direction and the elimination of the problem. Policy information in various campus publications is necessary, but normally these, especially the student handbooks, do not include all details that other forms of educational material might contain. A notable exception is Memphis State University, which prints its entire sexual harassment policy in the schedule of classes each semester along with its other policies such as its position on drug and alcohol use by students (1992).

A number of institutions have produced brochures that state the policy of the schools, the procedures for redress, and a list of those on campus who may be contacted to make a complaint. These materials are provided to all new students and are made available in various campus places. It should be emphasized that educational programs for students need to be offered on a frequent and ongoing basis given the high turnover rates of students, especially on two-year and commuting campuses, when compared with faculty and staff groups. Informal procedures to address the problem are spelled out—saying no or writing a letter to the harasser. The University of Iowa's policy statement clearly defines the task of education:

> *The Office of Affirmative Action is charged with distributing copies of this policy to all current members of the University community and to all those who join the community in the future. An annual letter from the Office of Affirmative Action will be sent to all faculty and staff to remind them of the contents of the University's Human Rights Policy, including the provisions added to it by this Policy. A copy of the Human Rights Policy will be included in student orientation materials, including those distributed to students in professional schools. In addition, copies of that Policy will be made continually available at appropriate campus centers and offices* (1991).

Merely addressing and discussing the subject of sexual harassment may cause some individuals to be more conscious of their behavior and discourage harassment. Paludi recommends discussion of sexual harassment in undergraduate and graduate courses, especially those dealing with human sexuality (1990). Procedures such as showing videos in classes or in commons areas of the campus and holding discussion groups for residence hall advisors or in student orientation programs also may be used. Some academic departments have produced their own anti-discrimination statements and distributed them to students; however, caution should be exercised to assure that departmental policy is in conformity with the overall institutional statement. Antioch University in Yellow Springs, Ohio, requires documentation of attendance in a sexual harassment education program before graduation (Mulhauser 1992). Stimson encourages training or discussion sessions that include helping women to understand that they can just refuse, and giving men and women alike lessons on gender and power (1989).

One of the most progressive programs of education is carried out by the City University of New York's Sexual Harassment Panel of Hunter College. This panel has been in operation since 1982, and its members have received special training for their positions. This group produces a number of resources for educating and preventing sexual harassment, one of which is a booklet titled *The Student in the Back Row: Avoiding Sexual Harassment in the Classroom* (Paludi 1990b). It is especially helpful for the professor who wants to become more sensitive to inadvertent sexual discrimination. The text begins:

> *The student in the back row may feel sexually harassed even though the professor has never made any advance or even a direct personal remark. The student may feel humiliated, embarrassed, or angry.*
>
> *IF the professor regularly tells jokes that present women as sex objects;*
> *OR habitually uses "he" or "his" to refer to students (even though 75 percent of Hunter's students are women);*
> *OR listens intently when a male student talks and responds to his remarks, but only smiles politely when a female student talks;*
> *OR makes derogatory remarks about gays and lesbians* (p. 281).

Providing such booklets for discussion in administrative and faculty meetings or simply distributing such materials to faculty and staff will increase awareness and may raise the sensitivity of faculty members.

Confidentiality

Investigating harassment claims is often a difficult task for educational institutions. The parties involved usually are members of the academic community. The college or university has an obligation to each person involved (Clark 1991), especially in the area of confidentiality. Before adopting a final policy and procedure to implement that policy, an institution would do well to consider the following in order to protect the privacy of all individuals to the maximum extent possible under the law.

As a general rule, information in the file of private institutions is not subject to public scrutiny. In contrast, state college and university officials may face questions about complaints of harassment and may be forced to reveal a significant amount of information—perhaps even the entire investigational file. The following guidelines may assist in maintaining confidentiality.

First, if the complaint involves actual or even potential criminal charges, information may be protected during the investigational stage. Second, medical records, including those of psychologists, generally are confidential. Third, records involving students normally are protected from disclosure under the Family Educational Rights and Privacy Act of 1974, commonly referred to as the Buckley Amendment (1974); however, at least one state court has determined that student records dealing with disciplinary matters are not protected from public scrutiny by that act (*Red and Black Publishing Co. Inc. et al. v. The Board of Regents et al.* 1993). Finally, a lawyer's files are almost always unavailable to the public or press, perhaps making it desirable to conduct investigations under the auspices of legal counsel. Even with these possible protections, a complainant should be made aware that, more than likely, her or his name and the nature of the complaint probably cannot be kept completely confidential.

Though confidentiality is important, it is suggested that some type of written records be maintained to identify repeat offenders. The College of Arts and Sciences at Cornell University in New York has adopted a procedure for identifying professors who repeatedly harass students. Students with complaints speak with one of two tenured faculty—one male and one female—who are sexual harassment counselors, appointed by the dean. After the counselor determines whether the complaint has merit (even if formal charges are not filed), a record of the complaint is kept in a "locked box" to which only the two counselors have access. This provides the institution with a memory while preserving confidentiality (National Association for Women In Education 1992).

Additional Considerations

While the elements discussed previously will provide an institution with a good sexual harassment policy, several other concerns surface in the literature that may produce an even better policy. Several sources recommend surveys of faculty, staff, and students on a periodic basis to assess the frequency and magnitude of the sexual harassment problem on individual campuses and to document the effectiveness of current educational programs (Wagner 1990; American Council on Education 1986; Association of American Colleges 1980). Such surveys serve to keep the issue of sexual harassment in the minds of the faculty and students and remind would-be perpetrators that the institution is alert to the problem.

ACE provides a list of 17 guidelines that may assist in improving existing sexual harassment policies or in designing new ones (1993). The association recommends that "additional training should be provided for supervisory personnel, especially deans, department heads, and administrative and student affairs staff, through workshops and seminars. Student and collegiate governance structures may be appropriate outlets for ongoing training and discussion" (p. 3). Hindus suggests that students and staff may find themselves more comfortable with peer counselors and peer support groups than a faculty or administrative representative (1990).

A good policy on sexual harassment also should take into account where policies that have been challenged in a court of law have faltered. Adams and Abarbanel suggest six such potential soft spots in sexual assault policies:

- Negligence due to "serious deficiencies in training, manpower, equipment, and morale" of a college security force;
- Inadequate prevention, if assault was "foreseeable";

- Misrepresentation to students and parents "that the campus was reasonably safe and that no unusual steps needed to be taken to ensure safety from violent assaults";
- Substandard facilities and care compared with standards required by states in landlord-tenant relationships or motel safety;
- Inadequate campus lighting; and
- Disciplining a student, faculty, or staff member for an alleged offense without providing for adequate due process (cited in Mulhauser 1992, p. 7).

While these deficiencies pertain more specifically to sexual assault than to sexual harassment, the implicit signal to campuses is to acknowledge the problem, take whatever precautions necessary to ensure the protection of the members of the university community, and have well-trained personnel in place to handle offenses if they occur.

A final consideration for campus groups developing sexual harassment policies and procedures has to do with the restoration of the reputation of an acquitted alleged perpetrator. In cases where accusations are brought against an individual, especially when the accusations have been made public, efforts should be made to correct the misperceptions and misinformation.

The Effectiveness of Sexual Harassment Policies

Although institutions of higher education have broadly adopted and operationalized campus-based policies for reporting and reducing the frequency of sexual harassment, few colleges and universities have systematically examined the effectiveness of such policies and the resultant practice (Robertson, Dyer, and Campbell 1988). Are these policies working? Or, as observed by Leatherman, "The common thread running through the policies is their failure to do the job" (1991, p. 1).

Williams, Lam, and Shively write of a University of Massachusetts at Amherst study that examines the impact of that institution's sexual harassment policy on reported prevalence of sexual harassment of undergraduate students (1992). The research also examines female undergraduates' awareness of the policy.

Following the implementation of the policy during the fall of 1982, surveys were conducted among random samples of female undergraduates using telephone interviews in 1983,

1986, and 1989. All three surveys utilized a 10-item question-naire addressing undergraduate women's experiences with sexual harassment by faculty and staff. The study data illustrate a steady decline over the study period in the proportion of students experiencing sexually harassing behavior and year-to-year decreases in the reported levels of nearly all 10 of the behaviors that were the primary focus of the study. The researchers conclude, " . . . the evidence suggests that the observed decline in reports of sexual harassment of women students by University faculty and staff represents a real change in the behavior of University employees, and this change most likely occurred in response to the University's sexual harassment policy and grievance procedure" (p. 61).

The authors further observe that the educational efforts con-ducted pursuant to the policy appear to have increased female students' awareness of sexual harassment issues, with a major-ity of respondents indicating awareness of the illegality of sex-ual harassment (87.6 percent, 91.1 percent, and 94.3 percent for the three years of the study period). In addition, there were year-to-year increases in the percentages of women reporting awareness of university policy and grievance proce-dures. In 1983, 38.1 percent of the students were aware of the general policy, and 30.7 percent were aware of the griev-ance procedures. These figures increased to 66.9 percent and 42.1 percent in 1986 and remained stable in 1989.

In contrast to these findings, researchers at Oklahoma State University report on surveys of undergraduate and graduate student populations that were conducted to ascertain whether the incidence and types of sexual harassment had changed following implementation of policy and educational efforts (McKinney and Howard 1986; McKinney, Olson, and Satter-field 1988). The authors conclude in both studies that despite aggressive eradication efforts, the incidence of harassment was as great or greater than reported prior to the policy adop-tion. They further report that, following more than three years of policy operation, one-half of the student respondents were unaware of the policy's existence, whereas only one-third knew how to report a sexual harassment incident.

The efficacy of institutional sexual harassment policies is further challenged by Biaggio, Watts, and Brownell: "Univer-sity policies may impede rather than facilitate processing of harassment complaints. If, as the U.S. Merit Systems Protection Board recommends, a good monitoring system is in place, then there is a means to document inadequacies in the policy and to revise the policy accordingly. If a monitoring system is not in place, then the responsibility for evaluating the policy is diffused and there may be no means to address inadequacies in the policy" (1990, p. 216). The authors further suggest that university procedures may militate against effective disposal of complaints because harassment complaints may be embarrassing to the institution and carry with them potential legal claims.

In a report by the Indiana University Office of Women's Affairs of a 1984 survey of institutions of higher learning (N=311) concerning policies and procedures developed to deal with sexual harassment (Robertson, Dyer, and Campbell 1988), the authors discuss the effectiveness of these policies and procedures. They state, "According to our results, then, harassers have little to fear from present sexual harassment grievance procedures, which often lack definitive means of discouraging harassing behaviors or redressing student complaints" (p. 801). They further observed that, as a result of heightened levels of awareness, institutions with sexual harassment policies and procedures reported more estimated and actual complaints than institutions without such policies. In spite of this evidence they draw this discouraging conclusion: "Nevertheless, since most felt that most complaints were not reported and few kept statistics, the conviction that sexual harassment policies and grievance procedures reduce sexual harassment by increasing complaints remains insufficiently supported by hard evidence" (p. 801).

Olswang critiques the very protracted and difficult experiences encountered by the University of Washington with the enforcement of a long-established university procedure for a violation of its sexual harassment policy (1992). In this case, a woman student filed a complaint with university officials in 1989 that she had been subjected to a series of unwanted and unwelcome sexual requests and improper touches by a senior faculty member. After years of hearings, appeals, and settled litigation, the matter is not yet fully resolved. The university settled litigation with the student by facilitating her completion of a degree at another institution and by paying substantial damages, costs, and attorney's fees. The accused professor was reinstated by the university's president.

The author offers this assessment of the experience: "The

obvious fallout from this process on both institutional reputation and institutional operation is significant. The disruption in the academic unit from which this faculty member and student came, with its faculty and students taking sides and acting as witnesses, has been devastating" (p. 53).

Clearly, we know little about the impact of institutional policies for the elimination of sexual harassment on campuses. A great deal of empirical study must be accomplished in a variety of institutional settings, focusing upon the full range of victims, harassers, and other members of academic communities. The outcomes of this research should provide academic institutions with more definitive direction as they seek to revise and improve the effectiveness of their sexual harassment policies.

How Have Higher Education Professional Associations Responded?

Many professional associations connected with the higher education community have taken action dealing with the topic of sexual harassment. Such action ranges from statements regarding their own position on the topic to recommendations for individual institutions to follow in the development of campus-specific policies and procedures. Several notable organizations are described below.

In 1984, AAUP adopted a position paper on sexual harassment, calling it a failure of professional ethics and academic freedom. Sexual harassment is defined as: (1) an unprofessional academic or work environment interfering with learning, job responsibilities, and future career opportunities; (2) abusive conduct that creates or implies discrimination toward personal or professional interests because of gender; and (3) sexual favors asked under the circumstance that the response determines academic or personnel decisions.

Procedures for bringing a complaint to the grievance officer should be confidential, with no written record. If the complainant decides to proceed, written statements are initiated by the complainant, and written copies are given by the grievance officer to the involved parties. The grievance officer may attempt to resolve the matter, or the complainant may proceed to a review by a faculty committee if the alleged offender is a faculty member. This committee may conduct its own inquiry; if sanctions are recommended against the faculty member, the grievance officer then submits the recommendations to the chief administrative officer or her/his designate (American Association of University Professors 1990a).

The National Association of College and University Business Officers (NACUBO), an organization that would typically relate to non-faculty employees, reiterates the EEOC's recommendations that higher education institutions have a written policy of disapproval of sexual harassment, sanctions including termination, training of all employees, and procedures for employees to file complaints (National Association of College and University Business Officers 1992). Such a stance ensures that a consistent message is sent to all segments of the college or university community.

The American Association of State Colleges and Universities (AASCU) Committee on Academic and Student Personnel condemns acts of sexual harassment, noting the positive need for trust between students and faculty and the negative effects of sexual harassment on the recruitment, appointment, and advancement processes on the institution (1981). AASCU generally recommends the establishment of a policy prohibiting sexual harassment and suggests that grievance procedures may have both informal and formal components.

In 1986, ACE developed a position paper on sexual harassment that is widely used as a standard by its members. ACE called upon the ethical obligation of colleges and universities to provide, for the good of the entire academic community, an environment free of verbal, physical, and visual sexual harassment and from the fear that it may occur. During 1993, ACE introduced a revised model for campus-based sexual harassment policies. While this document, "Sexual Harassment on Campus," has not been available for a sufficient period of time to have substantial impact among institutions of higher education, it does indicate the high level of interest ACE continues to devote to the issue. ACE President Robert Atwell, in a letter accompanying the statement, says, "This issue warrants your institution's utmost concern as the national debate on sexual harassment demonstrates" (National Association of College and University Business Officers 1992, p. 32).

The Southern Association of College Student Affairs Sexual Abuse Task Force developed a guidebook for use in sexual abuse educational programming and policy development (1990). It is geared primarily to student sexual harassment and includes samples of brochures and policies used by several Southern colleges and universities as well as available

"The disruption in the academic unit from which this faculty member and student came . . . has been devastating."

resources and an annotated bibliography.

While these associations do not have the power to enforce these policies, they serve as powerful and influential opinion shapers. As sexual harassment becomes the focus of conversations, debates, and discussions within them, the norms for individual and institutional behaviors can be influenced.

MODEL SEXUAL HARASSMENT POLICY AND PROCEDURE

Effective policies and procedures for dealing with sexual harassment in academic communities are regarded as a necessity and must be adapted to the administrative structures and academic climates of particular institutions. In addition, institutional policies and procedures must preserve the rights and privacy of both the accused and the accuser to the extent allowed by law.

The following model policies and procedures as illustrated by the accompanying flow chart and narrative incorporate elements from a variety of campus policies; however, the basic structure and language are derived from the University of Iowa's policy on sexual harassment (1991).

Rationale

Sexual harassment is reprehensible conduct that will not be tolerated by the institution. Sexual harassment subverts the mission of the institution and threatens the careers, educational experience, and well-being of students, faculty, and staff. It undermines authority and collegial relationships and generates suspicion, conflict, and ill feelings.

Relationships involving sexual harassment or discrimination on the basis of gender have no place within the educational community. In both obvious and subtle ways, sexual harassment is destructive to individual students, faculty, staff, and the academic community as a whole. When through fear of reprisal a student, faculty member, or staff member submits to or is pressured to submit to unwanted sexual attention, the institution's ability to carry out its mission is threatened. The enduring of an unwelcome hostile environment by students, faculty, and staff is not conducive to scholarly pursuits.

Sexual harassment is especially serious when it threatens relationships between teacher and student or supervisor and subordinate. In such situations, sexual harassment exploits unfairly the power inherent in a faculty member's or staff supervisor's position. Through grades, wage increases, recommendation for graduate study, performance evaluations, promotion, and the like, a teacher or supervisor can have a decisive influence on a student's, staff member's, or faculty member's career at the educational institution.

Although sexual harassment most often takes place in a situation that involves a "power differential" between the persons involved, the institution also recognizes that sexual harassment may occur between persons of the same institu-

FIGURE 1

MODEL SEXUAL HARASSMENT
COMPLAINT RESOLUTION PROCEDURE FOR
COLLEGES AND UNIVERSITIES

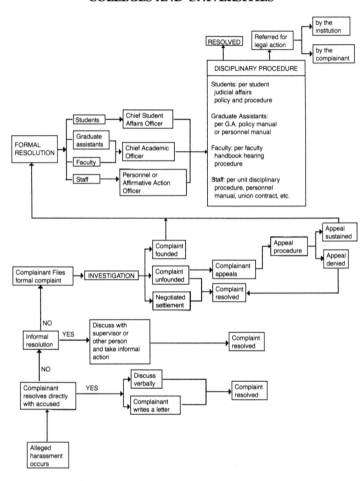

tional status. The institution will not tolerate behavior between or among members of the educational community that creates an unacceptable environment.

Prohibited Acts

No member of the educational community shall engage in sexual harassment. For the purpose of this policy, sexual harassment is defined as unwelcome or unwanted advances, requests for sexual favors, or other verbal or physical conduct of a sexual nature when:

- Submission to or toleration of such conduct is made explicitly or implicitly a term or condition of an individual's employment, promotion, performance evaluation, or status in a course, program, or activity; or
- Submission to or toleration of such conduct is used as a basis for an employment or educational decision affecting such individual; or
- Such conduct has the purpose or effect of unreasonably interfering with an individual's work or educational performance, or creating an intimidating, hostile, or offensive environment for work or learning.

Examples of Sexual Harassment
Sexual harassment includes any interpersonal attention of a sexual nature that is unwanted and unwelcome. Examples may include, but are not limited to, the following:

- Physical assault; assault in this sense includes any physical touching of any kind that is sexual in nature; or
- Direct or implied threats that submission to sexual advances may favorably affect employment, work status, promotion, grades, or letters of recommendation; or that rejection of sexual advances may negatively affect the same; or
- Direct propositions of a sexual nature; or
- Subtle pressure for sexual activity, one element of which may be conduct such as repeated and unwanted staring; or
- A pattern of conduct (not legitimately related to the subject matter of the course if a course is involved or to employment if employment is involved) that tends to bring discomfort and or humiliation, which may include comments of a sexual nature, or sexually explicit jokes, statements, questions, or anecdotes; or
- A pattern of conduct that would tend to bring discomfort or humiliation to a reasonable person at whom the conduct was directed, which may include unnecessary touching, patting, hugging, or brushing against a person's body; remarks of a sexual nature regarding a person's clothing

or body; or remarks about sexual activity or speculations about previous sexual experience.

Isolated and Inadvertent Minor Offenses

Members of the academic community who, without establishing a pattern of doing so, engage in isolated conduct that may tend to bring discomfort and/or humiliation as described above or who exhibit a pattern of engaging in such conduct but fail to reasonably realize that their actions tend to bring discomfort and/or humiliation demonstrate insensitivity that necessitates remedial measures. When administrators become aware that such activities are occurring in their area of responsibility, they should direct those engaged in such conduct to undertake an educational program designed to help them understand the harm done by such activities.

If, after participating in the educational program (or failing to participate after being directed to do so), a person continues to engage in the conduct described above, this person will be deemed to have engaged in such conduct as a deliberate pattern of behavior.

Consensual Relationships

For the purpose of this policy, the term "faculty" or "faculty member" shall include all of those who teach in the institution. This includes graduate assistants with teaching responsibilities as well as other instructional personnel.

The institution's educational mission is promoted by professionalism in faculty-student relationships. This professionalism is fostered by an atmosphere of mutual trust and respect. Actions of students and faculty members that tend to harm this atmosphere undermine professionalism and hinder fulfillment of the institution's mission. Trust and respect are diminished when those in positions of authority abuse, or appear to abuse, their power. Those who abuse, or appear to abuse, their power in such a context violate their duty to the academic community.

Faculty members exercise power over students, whether in giving them grades, praise, or criticism, evaluating them or making recommendations for future employment, or conferring other benefits on them. Amorous relationships between students and faculty members are obviously wrong when the faculty member has professional responsibility for, and thus power over, the student. Such situations greatly increase the probability that the faculty member will abuse this power and sexually exploit the student.

Given the fundamentally asymmetric nature of, and the "power differential" inherent in such relationships, any appearance of voluntary consent on the part of the student is suspect. Moreover, other students and faculty members may be affected by such unprofessional behavior because it places the faculty member in a position to advance or favor one student's interests at the expense of others, and implicitly makes obtaining benefits contingent on amorous or sexual favors.

The institution may therefore view it as unethical for faculty members to engage in amorous relationships with students who are enrolled in their classes or subject to their supervision, even when both parties appear to have consented to the relationship.

Consensual Relationships Within the Instructional Context

No faculty member shall have an amorous relationship (consensual or otherwise) with any student who is enrolled in a course being taught by the faculty member, or whose academic work (including work as a teaching assistant) is being supervised by the faculty member.

Consensual Relationships Outside the Instructional Context

Amorous relationships between students and faculty members, even those occurring outside the instructional context, are suspect by nature and may lead to difficulties. Particularly when the student and the faculty member are in the same academic unit or in units that are academically allied, relationships both parties view as consensual may appear to others to be exploitative.

Further, in such situations (and in others that may occur in the future, which neither party can anticipate), the faculty member may face serious conflicts of interest. In certain instances, it may be necessary for a faculty member to withdraw from participation in activities or decisions that tend to reward or penalize the student involved. A faculty member who fails to recognize such conflicts of interest and withdraw accordingly may reward or penalize a student with whom the faculty member has had an amorous relationship. In such cases, the faculty member has violated her or his ethical obligations to the student, to colleagues, and to the institution. Moreover, actions that occur after the breakup of such relationships may cause problems; e.g., the lack of a favorable recommendation for the student from the faculty mentor may be viewed as retaliation for "breaking up" and may be actionable.

Complaint Resolution Procedure

The following represents the procedure for resolving incidents where sexual harassment has been alleged. It corresponds to the flow chart (See Figure 1), which reads from bottom to top.

Alleged harassment occurs

When a minor incident involving sexual harassment occurs, the victim may be inclined to ignore it or offer minimal protest in the hope that the offensive behavior will cease and not be repeated. In general, this is an ineffective method of resolving such problems. Even if the behavior should cease in this particular relationship, there remains the probability that it represents a pattern of behavior on the part of the accused and that it has been or will be repeated in other relationships. At the very least, the accused may retain the belief that such behavior is acceptable. For this reason (if for no other), the victim should take steps to resolve the matter conclusively and finally.

Complainant resolves with person involved

Initially, the victim may attempt to resolve the issue directly with the accused. This attempt need not be confrontational in nature. It may involve speaking directly to the accused (either face-to-face or by telephone) or writing a letter to the accused.

It should be noted that writing a letter also establishes an initial level of documentation of the incident (albeit from the victim's perspective) and an effort to resolve it. If this method of resolution is chosen, it is recommended that a third party (such as a colleague or faculty advisor) accompany the victim when hand-delivering the letter to the accused; the third party need not know the contents of the letter but can provide independent verification that a letter was delivered on a particular date should further action become necessary.

A verbal attempt at resolution may also provide initial documentation if a written record of the conversation is made and kept by the complainant.

In either case, the complainant should include the following points in communicating with the accused either verbally or in writing:

1. The date, time, and place the incident of harassment occurred.
2. The specific behavior of the accused which the complainant found offensive.
3. The effect the behavior had on the complainant—specifically, how the complainant felt (e.g., embarrassed, uncomfortable, humiliated, etc.) and what the real consequence was—what the complainant did or considered doing as a result of feeling this way (e.g., dropped a class, performed poorly on an exam, paper, or work assignment, lost sleep, had difficulty concentrating). This element need not dwell too heavily on feelings, even though including feelings is important; this element should focus on the real consequences the behavior had on the victim.
4. The specific action the complainant expects. Usually, this involves only a statement that the behavior must cease and not be repeated. In some cases, this may include a request that a personnel performance evaluation or a class grade be changed or at least withdrawn until a fair resolution can be reached.

Note that any attempt at direct resolution between victim and accused should be regarded as strictly voluntary on the part of the complainant. No policy and procedure should include a requirement for this to be the initial step in resolution of the complaint. The complainant always must have the right to proceed directly to informal resolution with a third party or even to lodge a formal complaint without being required to attempt to resolve the complaint directly with the accused. At this stage, issues of legality, evidence, and due process do not arise. However, resolving the complaint at this stage may have the advantage of avoiding public confrontation, attempts at retaliation, and publicity. It also may give the accused a new perspective on the harm caused by such behavior and allow the accused to cease such behavior while not being adjudicated guilty.

An effort at direct resolution probably is not appropriate where the alleged offense involved force or threat of force.

Informal resolution

In this step, the complainant confers with a third party in an effort to resolve the complaint. This also establishes an initial level of documentation in that the alleged offense is now known to another person. The person to whom the complaint is brought may be the complainant's supervisor, the accused's supervisor, or a member of the institution's counseling staff. This person should have the right to defer this responsibility to another person if he or she feels unable to perform this task effectively.

In some instances, a person may be officially designated by the administration to perform this duty (e.g., an affirmative action officer). In such an arrangement, the individual assigned this duty should receive special training in resolving such complaints.

The person to whom the complaint is brought would discuss the incident with the complainant and document all the facts and circumstances surrounding the allegations. The person then would counsel the complainant as to all the options available under this policy. The person then might assist the complainant in resolving the complaint informally or might present suggestions or guidelines for drafting a formal complaint.

The person to whom the complaint is brought will not initially inform the accused of the complainant's action without the consent of the complainant. However, the complainant's name ultimately must be revealed to the accused by the person to whom the complaint is brought. Although the identity of the complainant is probably known to the accused once the proceedings begin to unravel, the complainant may be only one of several victims, others of whom may not have brought complaints. Maintaining privacy in this way also may help in resolving other incidents as well, and the privacy of the victim is preserved to the extent possible.

The investigational and/or hearing proceedings also should remain confidential to the extent allowed by law. The person to whom the complaint is brought should regard it as a trust not to discuss the matter with anyone not directly involved in the resolution of the complaint.

In the event that the third party is able, through discussion, to resolve the matter to the satisfaction of all persons involved, the matter may be closed at this point. It may be that the accused will acknowledge fault and agree that the behavior will not be repeated, and/or that the victim will be satisfied that the matter is resolved. The third party should maintain a confidential record of the complaint and its resolution in the event the behavior recurs.

Similarly, an attempt at third-party resolution of sexual harassment complaints should not be a requirement unless there is a person officially designated by the administration to handle such responsibilities. In the absence of such a designated official, the complainant must always have the right to proceed directly to a formal complaint without being required to attempt to resolve the complaint through a third party. (For other options for informal resolutions, see earlier discussion.)

The complainant may be only one of several victims, others of whom may not have brought complaints.

Formal complaint

A formal complaint may be filed with the institutional official designated to handle such complaints (e.g., the office of affirmative action). The investigator will obtain all necessary details and consult with the appropriate administrative officer to determine how best to investigate or handle the incident. At this juncture, it is necessary to consult with the institution's legal counsel.

The purpose of the investigation is to establish whether there is a reasonable basis for believing that the alleged violation of this policy has occurred. The investigation may involve oral interviews and/or written statements from the complainant, the accused, and any witnesses who may be able to provide pertinent information about the facts of the case. At all times, confidentiality of the proceedings will be maintained to the extent allowed by law.

In the course of the investigation, the accused will be afforded a full opportunity to respond to the allegations. The results of the investigation may fall into three categories:

1. Unfounded: If the complaint is determined to be unfounded (i.e., a probability exists that the offense did not occur and/or that the accused did not commit the offense), the complaint usually will be regarded as resolved. However, the victim may have the right to appeal this decision to a higher authority. In this case, the person designated would review all materials and make the final determination as to whether to sustain the appeal (refer the case to the cognizant administrator) or deny the appeal (matter resolved).

2. Negotiated Settlement: In some cases, the filing of a formal complaint and investigation may result in an opportunity for a negotiated settlement of the case. Analagous to a "consent decree," such a settlement might not involve an official determination as to whether a case was founded or unfounded and might not involve an admission of guilt on the part of the accused. However, an agreement by all parties to resolve the matter under certain negotiated conditions might be sufficient to preclude further official action.
3. Founded: If the complaint is determined to be founded (i.e., a probability exists that the offense occurred as represented and that the accused committed the offense), the matter will be referred to the cognizant administrator for formal action.

Formal action

If, after the results of the investigation are reviewed, the complaint is determined to be founded, it will be referred to the cognizant administrator for resolution. The resolution process may be different depending upon the category of the person(s) involved. For example:

- If the accused is a student, the matter may be referred to the chief student affairs officer for resolution as per the appropriate judicial affairs policies and procedures. If the accused is a graduate assistant, the matter may be referred to the chief academic officer for resolution as per appropriate policies regarding graduate assistants.
- If the accused is a faculty member, the matter may be referred to the chief academic officer for resolution as per the hearing procedure for faculty discipline.
- If the accused is a staff member, the matter may be referred to the director of personnel for handling as per institutional policy and procedure, to the unit administrator for handling as per unit disciplinary procedure, or handled as per collective bargaining agreement, if any.

Any appeal would be handled as defined by appropriate disciplinary procedures. In addition to internal disciplinary procedures, the matter might be referred for legal action (either civil or criminal) by either the complainant or the institution.

Protection of Rights

Investigations of complaints will be initiated only with the complainant's informed consent. As the investigation proceeds, the accused may not be initially, but at the appropriate time, must be informed of the allegations, the identity of the complainant, and the facts surrounding the allegations.

The complainant will be informed fully of steps taken during the investigation, following which both parties will be informed of the facts developed in the course of the investigation. Additionally, both parties will be promptly informed about the final outcome of the proceedings and be afforded the opportunity to read and copy the pertinent files.

To the extent possible, all proceedings will be conducted in a way calculated to protect the confidentiality interests of both parties. Moreover, all reasonable action will be taken to ensure that the complainant and those testifying on behalf of the complainant will suffer no retaliation as a result of their actions. Steps to see that retaliation is avoided might include:

- Lateral transfers of one or more of the parties in an employment setting or a comparable move if a classroom setting is involved; and
- Arrangements that academic and/or employment evaluations concerning the complainant or others be made by an appropriate individual other than the accused.

In the event that the allegations are not substantiated, all reasonable steps will be taken to restore the reputation of the accused if it may have been damaged by the proceedings. If a complainant is found to have been intentionally dishonest in making the allegations or to have made allegations maliciously, the complainant is subject to institutional discipline.

Educational Programs: Education as an Instrument of Institutional Policy

Educational efforts in the area of sexual harassment are essential to the establishment of a campus environment that is as free as possible of sexual harassment and where high standards of conduct in consensual relationships are observed. At least four goals may be achieved through such education:

1. Ensuring that all victims and potential victims are aware of their rights;

2. Notifying all members of the campus community of that conduct that is proscribed by the policy;
3. Informing administrators of the proper procedures for addressing complaints of violations of the policy; and
4. Helping to educate insensitive individuals about the problems the policy addresses.

Preparation and dissemination of information

An institutional administrator is charged with distributing copies of the policy to all current members of the campus community and to all those who join the community in the future. A periodic notice will be sent to all faculty and staff to remind them of the policy. A copy of the policy will be included in the materials distributed at new-student orientation, and copies of the policy will continually be made available at appropriate campus centers and offices.

A designated campus administrator will develop training programs for persons who are likely to receive complaints that this policy has been violated, including but not limited to such people as residence hall advisors, academic advisors, and staff supervisors. Academic departments are encouraged to provide training sessions for graduate assistants and other instructional personnel.

A designated campus administrator will develop a training course designed to inform those who inadvertently violate the policy of the problems associated with their insensitive conduct. The course shall be mandated for those found to have committed isolated or inadvertent offenses and may be an element of a negotiated settlement of a complaint. It also may be mandated for persons found to have violated the policy, with or without the imposition of other sanctions.

The Role of Governing Boards and Administrators in Eliminating Sexual Harassment

The governing boards of America's colleges and universities are charged with the responsibilities for overall institutional policy development and for the assessment and maintenance of the quality of academic programs. Trustee responsibility must be clearly exercised if the specter of sexual harassment is to be eliminated. Mulhauser has suggested that failure of trustees to act may "expose our colleges to costly and unnecessary litigation" (p. 11). She further suggests that boards of governance are obligated to do the following:

1. Inform ourselves about campus policies related to sexual offenses and sex discrimination as well as federal and state laws prohibiting discrimination on the basis of gender. Continually work to improve these policies.
2. Require appropriate campus education programs.
3. Ensure that policies protect the rights of the accused as well as the accuser (1992, p. 11).

Kirby, Murrell, and Riggs (1992) write that trustees should seek to ensure that their institutions are prepared to meet the challenges of sexual harassment by responding to these questions:

- Does your institution have a policy unequivocally prohibiting sex discrimination and sexual harassment?
- Does your institution have a sexual harassment grievance procedure that is well-publicized, easily accessible, and included in your student and faculty handbooks?
- Does your institution provide professional training for your affirmative action officer or other staff member responsible for implementing the grievance procedure and see that he or she is well-informed regarding the basic requirements of the federal and state law? Is this individual trained to deal sensitively with the needs and difficulties of persons bringing charges?
- Does your institution conduct workshops for faculty, staff, and student groups to increase awareness of these policies and procedures? Do the workshops provide concrete information concerning the nature of "hostile environment" sexual harassment?
- Are steps taken to ensure that such workshops do not deteriorate into sessions on mere technical observance of the policy's requirements?
- Are you satisfied with your institution's policy regarding consensual relationships between faculty or staff and students? Is there acknowledgment that when such relationships turn sour upon termination they often spawn sexual harassment charges?
- Is the institution's published procedure scrupulously followed when a student or employee lodges a claim of sex discrimination against the institution or its staff? Are all actions that discourage an individual's claim or foster an extra-procedural "quiet settlement" clearly forbidden?

• Have you reviewed all programs that are sexually segregated (i.e., athletics, fraternity, and sorority support programs) or that tend to benefit one gender more than another with a view toward ensuring equity?

College and university administrators share with governing board members responsibility to exercise leadership in the elimination of sexual harassment from academic communities. In addition to the expectations cited for board members, institutional leaders should: (1) periodically remind all members of the academic community of institutional policies on sexual harassment; (2) establish policies that define sexual misconduct clearly and firmly and state that such misconduct will not be tolerated; (3) provide periodic education directed to the elimination of sexual harassment; (4) make all members of the academic community aware of avenues for seeking redress and actions that will be taken against individuals violating sexual harassment policies; and (5) create a climate in which sexual harassment cannot exist. The creation of such a climate is the focus of the final chapter of this report.

FROM CONFLICT TO COMMUNITY

The language of sexual harassment is a language of conten-
tiousness. It is replete with legalities, conflict, adversarial relationships, and inequality. It tends to separate, to pit one person or one gender against another, and to devolve into issues
of power, dominance, conquest, hierarchy, winning, and losing. Words like victim, perpetrator, sanctions, and offender
are more commonly thought of in the context of the legal
system or the courts than in the groves of academe. Yet, the
foregoing discussion jolts us into the reality that the tranquility
of the ivory tower has been disturbed, that the idyllic environment that so many of its inhabitants have enjoyed for years
has not been so idyllic for many others. Just as flaws have
been discovered in society generally in terms of gender inequities and abuses, so have they been discovered in our colleges and universities. One of the most insidious of these is
sexual harassment.

From conflict to community. How would administrators
and governing boards, faculty and staff, students, and support
personnel begin to craft an environment that would be free
of the damaging—often paralyzing—effects of sexual harassment? How could we foster a climate that would enable all
persons to learn, work, grow, and develop to their highest
potential? How can we honor differences in roles and responsibilities without abuses of power and denigration of human
dignity? How can we move to right the balance of power,
ameliorate the innate structural inequalities, and replace the
culture of dependence with an ethic of care?

William Carey, writing about the U.S. Navy following the
1991 Tailhook Convention in Las Vegas, stated, "The problem
is institutional. So long as the Navy is segregated by gender,
harassment will not go away. . . . It creates a culture, a lifestyle
and a mindset that has to be understood to put the events
. . . into some context. . . . As long as the Navy is segregated
by gender, it will continue to have a disproportionate amount
of problems between the sexes" (1992, p. A11). What Carey
is describing is a structural inequity required by law; the system has a built-in power differential that results in a culture
of dependence where those in a lesser position are always
dependent on those with more power.

Although the inequity in higher education is not congres-
sionally mandated, as is the case with the U.S. Navy, the academy also remains essentially gender-segregated. In spite of
statutes prohibiting discrimination and the resulting affirma-

tive action efforts, nationwide, in 1988, men still made up 73 percent and women 27 percent of the faculty (Russell et al. 1988). The fact remains that in the top administrative ranks, the female point of view is still often missing, as only 12 percent of college and university presidents are female (American Council on Education 1992). Administrative leaders must move to truly open all positions to women, to fill them with qualified women when possible, and to make a commitment to mentor and develop women for leadership roles.

Without a critical mass of women in decision-making positions, the female voice is drowned. Only when there is a reasonable gender balance are women free to consistently contribute to the dialogue in a sustained way. Johnson and Schulman (1989) report·that women are increasingly disadvantaged as their numbers in a group decrease, and Rosabeth Moss Kanter, author of *Women and Men in the Corporation* (1977), wrote of the importance of a critical mass of the minority group, whether it be in terms of gender or race. The removal of structural barriers and the commitment to increased numbers of women in positions of responsibility will, it is hoped, result in a distribution and sharing of power that can reduce the potential for abuse.

Role of Administrators

In addition to affirmative action policies and actions to eliminate gender segregation, academic policy makers have a responsibility to provide leadership that ensures gender sensitivity in all other policies and practices. Sexual harassment policy, especially, should be collaboratively developed to reflect the female point of view. If such policies are decreed with no input from women, they are apt to overlook concerns or trivialize matters that are of major importance to that constituent group.

In addition to policy development and implementation, administrators also have a responsibility to set a tone for the institution and create a larger vision that transcends details. Boyer states that, while " . . . affirming principles surely will not resolve all differences of opinion, . . . [it will] help lift [the] level of discourse and provide a framework within which decisions can be made" (1990, p. 67). There will always be tension between this larger vision of a caring community and the rules and policies for its implementation. The realities of the regulations often seem reductionistic compared to the ideal of the dream. Nevertheless, the vision must be held up and championed. Chancellor Kenneth R.R. Gros Louis at Indiana University, Bloomington, exemplified this stance when he stated, "We must not back down in our attempts to create a climate in which the fundamental business of learning can go on unimpeded. We must make sure that we can guarantee basic needs and services, that we see the loss of personal safety—whether we mean sexual harassment or assault, racial harassment or assault . . . as . . . a basic assault, a personal, individual violation of the rights that we all have as citizens, as students, as faculty and staff" (quoted in Boyer, 1990, p. 44).

This determined adherence to the creation of a caring community also helps us to avoid relying only on a technical solution to a moral problem (Bellah et al. 1991). " . . . technical reason alone," such as is played out in laws, regulations, policies and rules, "is insufficient to manage our social difficulties or to make sense of our lives" (p. 44). Thus, while we may depend on technical solutions to guide us initially, eventually we must shift the responsibility to internal controls and develop models of integrity and authenticity for our interactions.

While we must work at increasing numbers of women in leadership roles, we also must work at changing attitudes. Parker Palmer has helped us to understand a dimension of this transformation that is particularly appropriate (1987). He credits feminist thought as one of the avenues through which a relational epistemology is being brought alongside the more predominant objectivism in higher education. He further posits that we cannot have a successful educational community without honoring both the objectivist and relational ways of knowing.

While a relational epistemology, one that is contextual, wholistic, and connected, is certainly not limited to women, nor is objectivism with its emphasis on abstractions, rational, and linear thinking limited to men, they do seem to be gender related in our culture. A respect and appreciation for the value of both avenues for accessing truth and the creative tension that results from their interplay enhance our capacity for community. Such attitudes are more likely to be developed in an atmosphere where the status of women is equal to that of men, and the full realization of women's scholarly potential is not likely to flourish on a campus where women fear harassment.

Administrative leaders in academic departments also have a role to play in bringing about changes in attitudes and practices and in creating a climate that discourages sexual harassment. As at higher administrative levels, to be effective, efforts must center not only on enacting policies, but on creating a climate that is free of gender inequality. As Sharon Howard states, "Where women are devalued . . . an atmosphere is created in which sexual harassment may flourish" (1991). Department chairs also have a direct responsibility for leadership in curriculum development and teaching—two important avenues that specifically impact on students.

Role of Curriculum

The curriculum represents a major vehicle for bringing about change in higher education. It constitutes the "what" that we teach, the content, the material that we choose to represent a discipline's method of inquiry and way of organizing knowledge. It has been under severe criticism during recent years, not only by women's groups, but by other under- or nonrepresented groups, for being predominantly male, white, and western. The curriculum, properly constructed, can be instrumental in developing an appreciation for the role of gender and other differences in our society without succumbing to a hierarchy.

Elizabeth Minnich writes of a curriculum in which women and men are represented as both similar and different—one in which those differences are recognized as a form of human richness (1989). She cautions that this cannot be accomplished by simply adding on courses such as "Counseling Women" or programs such as women's studies but must occur as the contributions and thinking of both men and women are woven throughout the field of study.

Courses and programs dealing specifically with women have played an invaluable part, however, in calling attention to the inequities in the curriculum, and their contribution in bringing about the paradigm shift that is occurring has been significant. As such programs have introduced more and more new information, it has become necessary to rethink and reconfigure the entire way of organizing and arranging knowledge.

Role of Teaching

As the curriculum changes, teaching practices also must change. Research during the past 20 years has provided an array of new theoretical developments that give increased insight into the way people learn and develop, suggesting the efficacy of using alternative teaching strategies to accommodate differences among students in our classes. Even the epistemologies of relatedness and connectedness addressed earlier call for different pedagogical approaches, demanding acknowledgment and valuing of the student's experience as a base of knowledge complementing other sources and breaking down traditional hierarchical modes of teaching (Schmitz 1992).

While some research indicates gender differences in learning style preferences (Kolb 1984), such distinctions may be a result of socialization and, as both men and women are exposed to and come to adopt more inclusive approaches, the differences may disappear.

A similar idea is developed in the book *Women's Ways of Knowing* (1986) in which Mary Belenky and her colleagues discuss separate and connected knowing. They stress that these modes may be gender-related, but that no hard data exist to indicate that they are gender-specific. Again, the inclusion of teaching methods that engender a respect and appreciation for the value of both avenues for accessing truth and the creative tension that results from their interplay and from attempts to integrate them enhance our capacity for community.

In addition to pedagogical changes driven by theoretical developments, many teaching practices need to be re-examined from the technical perspective as well. "The Student in the Back Row: Avoiding Sexual Harassment in the Classroom," (Paludi 1990), mentioned earlier, provides guidelines for avoiding behavior that is sexually harassing. Telling jokes that present women as sex objects, habitually using masculine pronouns to represent all people, or attending to male students more than to female students are among teacher behaviors that are regarded as inappropriate and that constitute gender harassment. Careful attention to all language—both verbal and non-verbal—in the classroom, both on their part as well as on the part of their students, helps teachers to con-

Many teaching practices need to be re-examined from the technical perspective as well.

vey a sensitivity and respect toward both men and women students. Such a stance is essential if the "chilly climate" reported by Sandler (1986) is to be eradicated.

Role of Student Services

Student services offer colleges and universities a premier opportunity to distribute information about sexual harassment, to engage in a dialogue about acceptable and unacceptable behaviors between men and women, and to explore and influence attitudes on gender. The Southern Association for College Student Affairs' guidebook, *Preventing Sexual Harassment and Sexual Assault,* offers guidelines for developing sexual harassment policies and grievance procedures as well as educational materials and programs (1990). Student affairs professionals often have more freedom in choosing "content" for programmatic efforts; they are not bound by rigid curricula and disciplinary constraints. Additionally, their area of interest and concern tends to reside more in the affective and personal dimension of the student's life rather than in the cognitive and intellectual domain. Thus, they perhaps have more freedom to deal with issues of immediate concern to the institution or to the students than classroom teachers may have.

For students residing on campus, seminars on sexual harassment fit nicely into ongoing programming efforts. Resident advisors should be trained to conduct discussion groups on the topic and to assist residents in processing and dealing with incidents. Further, they should be fully aware of policies and procedures for filing grievances and should be prepared to provide advocacy for students where needed.

Fraternities, sororities, and other social groups offer similar opportunities for presentations and dialogue about acceptable and unacceptable behavior between men and women. Such groups have often been the source of complaints and have been cited as one point of origin for unacceptable behavior, particularly peer harassment. Any campus subgroup provides the potential for educational opportunities, both for disseminating policy as well as for engendering attitudinal change.

Student services personnel also administer the procedure by which most campuses adjudicate student behavior problems. Harassment of any kind should be prohibited in student codes of conduct, and protocols for the resolution of disciplinary offenses should not be at odds with grievance procedures.

Counseling services for victims of harassment are most often provided by student affairs, and care should be taken that professional counselors are adequately trained in handling victims as required by the Campus Sexual Assault Victims' Bill of Rights. Counselors also may be involved in outreach and educational efforts, either as guests presenters in classes, residence halls, or in other group settings. They have the additional advantage of expertise in helping students work through questions and feelings that may surface during discussions of sexual harassment.

Other areas, such as health services, student orientation, and student activities, may also play a part in the elimination of sexual harassment. Any point of contact between university personnel and students offers an opportunity to convey an attitude of respect and regard.

Role of Athletics

Athletics is one of the most difficult areas in which colleges and universities must address the issue of sexual harassment and gender discrimination due to the financial ramifications and the influence of alumni and community groups. Even a definition of what is meant by parity for women in intercollegiate sports is yet to be universally embraced. Gender equity in college sports is mandated by Title IX of the Education Amendments of 1972, although interpretations of that mandate vary.

It is generally agreed that women and men should have an equal chance to participate in and benefit from collegiate athletic programs. Beyond that, the waters get murky. Individual institutions, sports conferences, the courts, and the National Collegiate Athletic Association (NCAA) have vested interests in the ultimate outcome of the debate. Actions range from the Big Ten conference's requirement that members seek a balance between the number of men and women who compete in their sports programs to considerations for member schools in other conferences to sponsor certain women's sports (Blum 1993).

The NCAA has designated a special panel to study the issue of gender-equity and submit a package of proposals at the 1994 convening of that association. Many schools and athletic conferences are awaiting recommendations from that group before taking action independent of the NCAA.

Since athletics was the most talked-about issue in the testimony in legislative hearings regarding Title IX, it is unlikely that the issue of the role of athletics in achieving gender parity in higher education will be settled soon. In the meantime, athletic teams, support groups such as cheerleaders, and the social activities that are associated with intercollegiate sports can and should be held to the same standards of conduct and respect for human dignity embraced by their sponsoring institutions.

Conclusion

Higher education institutions have been given a special role in our society. They are a major sociocultural force whose purpose is not only to transmit our heritage, but to shape the future as well. They are expected to respond to emerging sociological circumstances, to the inequities, and to the resulting disenfranchisement that many citizens feel. They have an obligation to embrace diversity and create a climate of inclusiveness. Most important, they have an obligation to provide a harassment-free environment in which students can learn, professors can pursue their teaching and scholarly activities, and other employees can carry out their responsibilities.

A major part of that responsibility lies in conducting research on the issue of sexual harassment. How effective are our sexual harassment policies? Do educational programs, both curricular and extra-curricular, decrease the incidence of sexual harassment? How does the presence of women in positions of responsibility alter the norms of the institution? Only as we look at our institutions critically and make the corrections that are indicated by our inquiry can we become the societal model that we should be.

By serving as moral exemplars in their communities, colleges and universities have an excellent opportunity to influence the opinions and actions of those agencies with which they do business and have relationships. In so doing, higher education can continue to fulfill its responsibility as a major formative institution in American society.

REFERENCES

The Educational Resources Information Center (ERIC) Clearinghouse on Higher Education abstracts and indexes the current literature on higher education for inclusion in ERIC's data base and announcement in ERIC's monthly bibliographic journal, *Resources in Education* (RIE). Most of these publications are available through the ERIC Document Reproduction Service (EDRS). For publications cited in this bibliography that are available from EDRS, ordering number and price code are included. Readers who wish to order a publication should write to the ERIC Document Reproduction Service, 7420 Fullerton Rd., Suite 110, Springfield, VA 22153-2852. (Phone orders with VISA or MasterCard are taken at 800-443-ERIC or 703-440-1400.) When ordering, please specify the document (ED) number. Documents are available as noted in microfiche (MF) and paper copy (PC). If you have the price code ready when you call EDRS, an exact price can be quoted. The last page of the latest issue of *Resources in Education* also has the current cost, listed by code.

Adams, A., and G. Abarbanel. 1992. *Sexual Assault on Campus: What Colleges Can Do.* Santa Monica, Calif.: Rape Treatment Center, Santa Monica Hospital Center.

Adams, J.W., J.L. Kotke, and J.S. Padgitt. 1983. "Sexual Harassment of University Students." *Journal of College Student Personnel* 24: 484-90.

Alliance Against Sexual Coercion. 1980. *University Grievance Procedures, Title IX, and Sexual Harassment on Campus.* Boston: Alliance Against Sexual Coercion.

American Association of State Colleges and Universities. June 1981. *Policy Statement on Sexual Harassment.* Washington, D.C.: American Association of State Colleges and Universities.

American Association of University Professors. 1990a. "Sexual Harassment: Suggested Policy and Procedures for Handling Complaints." In *Policy Documents and Reports,* 113-15. Washington, D.C.: American Association of University Professors.

———. September/October 1990b. "Sexual Harassment: Suggested Policy and Procedures for Handling Complaints." *Academe:* 42-43.

American Council on Education. December 1986. *Sexual Harassment on Campus: Suggestions for Reviewing Campus Policy and Educational Programs.* Washington, D.C.: American Council on Education.

———. April 1989. "Sexual Harassment." Unpublished newsletter. Washington, D.C.: American Council on Education.

———. 1992. *Women Chief Executive Officers in U.S. Colleges and Universities, Table XIII, April 15, 1992.* Washington, D.C.: American Council on Education, Office of Women in Higher Education.

———. 1993. "Sexual Harassment on Campus." Washington, D.C.: American Council on Education.

Association of American Colleges. "Policy Nixes Harassment and Faculty-Student Romance." *PSEW Update*, undated newsletter.

Association of American Colleges. 1980. "Title VII Sexual Harassment Guidelines and Educational Employment." Paper published by the Project on the Status and Education of Women. Washington, D.C.: Association of American Colleges. ED 200 097. 7 pp. MF–01; PC–01.

Bailey, N., and M. Richards. 1985. "Tarnishing the Ivory Tower: Sexual Harassment in Graduate Training Programs in Psychology." Los Angeles: Paper presented at the American Psychological Association.

Bayly, S. 1990. "Meritor and Related Cases." *Synthesis: Law and Policy in Higher Education*: 114-19.

Belenky, M.F, B.M. Clinchy, N.R. Goldberger, and J.M. Tarule. 1986. *Women's Ways of Knowing: The Development of Self, Voice, and Mind.* New York: Basic Books.

Bellah, R.N., R. Madsen, W.M. Sullivan, A. Swidler, and S.M. Tipton. 1991. *The Good Society.* New York: Alfred A. Knopf.

Benson, D.J., and G.E. Thompson. 1982. "Sexual Harassment on a University Campus: The Confluence of Authority Relations, Sexual Interest and Gender Stratification." *Social Problems* 29(3): 236-51.

Biaggio, M., D. Watts, and A. Brownell. 1990. "Addressing Sexual Harassment: Strategies for Prevention and Change." In *Ivory Power: Sexual Harassment on Campus,* edited by M. Paludi, 213-30. Albany: State University of New York Press.

Blum, D. January 13, 1993. "Athletic Conferences Struggle with Issue of Sex Equity." *The Chronicle of Higher Education* A: 34.

Bond, M. 1988. "Division 27 Sexual Harassment Survey: Definition, Impact and Environmental Context." *The Community Psychologist* 21: 7-10.

Boyer, E.L. 1990. *A Special Report. Campus Life: In Search of Community.* Princeton, N.J.: The Carnegie Foundation for the Advancement of Teaching.

Bradway, B. 1992. "Sexual Harassment: It's Not Hidden Anymore." *Survivor* 3: 2-4.

Brown, L.S. 1991. "Not Outside the Range: One Feminist Perspective on Psychic Trauma." *American Imago* 48: 119-33.

Burgess, A.W., and L.L. Holmstrom. 1979. "Adaptive Strategies and Recovery from Rape." *American Journal of Psychiatry* 136: 1,278-89.

The Bureau of National Affairs. March 26, 1992. *Affirmative Action Compliance Manual for Federal Contractors: News and Developments.* Washington, D.C.: The Bureau of National Affairs 57: 3-4.

Calhoun, K.S., and B.M. Atkeson. 1991. *Treatment of Rape Victims.* New York: Pergamon Press.

Carleton College. 1990. *Policy Against Sexual Harassment.* Northfield, Minn.: Carleton College, adopted June 21, 1990.

Carey, W.P. July 9, 1992. "Scolding Not Enough for Navy." *The Commercial Appeal* A: 11.

Clark, C. August 1991. "Sexual Harassment." *Congressional Quarterly Researcher* 539-55.

Connolly, W.B. Jr., and A.B. Marshall. 1989. "Sexual Harassment of University or College Students by Faculty Members." *Journal of College and University Law* 15(4): 381-403.

Cole, E., ed. 1990. *Sexual Harrassment on Campus: A Legal Compendium.* 2d ed. Washington, D.C.: National Association of College and University Attorneys.

Crull, P. 1982. "Stress Effects of Sexual Harassment on the Job: Implications for Counseling." *American Journal of Orthopsychiatry* 52: 539-44.

D'Ercole, A. 1988. "Sexual Harassment and Gender Issues in Community Psychology." *The Community Psychologist* 21: 22.

Dietz-Uhler, B., and A. Murrell. November 1992. "College Students' Perceptions of Sexual Harassment: Are Gender Differences Decreasing?" *Journal of College Student Development* 33: 540-46.

Dozier, J. 1990. "Sexual Harassment: It Can Happen Here." *AGB Reports* 32(1): 15-20.

Dziech, B.W. November 13, 1991. "Colleges Must Help to Unravel the Bewildering Complexities of Sexual Harassment." *The Chronicle of Higher Education*: B2.

Dziech, B.W., and L. Weiner. 1984. *The Lecherous Professor: Sexual Harassment on Campus.* Boston: Beacon Press.

Equal Employment Opportunity Commission. November 10, 1980. "Guidelines on Discrimination Because of Sex." Washington, D.C.: Equal Employment Opportunity Commission.

————. March 19, 1990. "Policy Guidance on Current Issues of Sexual Harassment," later published in part at 29 C.F.R. 1601 et al. (1991). Washington, D.C.: Equal Employment Opportunity Commission.

————. 1992. "Facts About Sexual Harassment." Washington, D.C.: Equal Employment Opportunity Commission.

Fitzgerald, L.F., and S. Shullman. August 1985. The development and validation of an objectively scored measure of sexual harassment. Paper presented at the annual meeting of the American Psychological Association, Los Angeles.

Fitzgerald, L., S. Shullman, N. Bailey, M. Richards, J. Swecker, Y. Gold, M. Ormerod, and L. Weitzman. 1988. "The Incidence and Dimensions of Sexual Harassment in Academia and the Workplace." *Journal of Vocational Behavior* 32: 152-75.

Fitzgerald, L.F., and L. Weitzman. 1988. "The Incidence and Dimensions of Sexual Harassment in Academia and the Workplace." *Jour-

nal of Vocational Behavior 32: 152-75.

Franklin, P., J. Moglin, P. Zatling-Boring, and R. Angress. 1981. *Sexual and Gender Harassment in the Academy.* New York: Modern Language Association.

Fuehrer, A., and K.M. Schilling. 1988. "Sexual Harassment of Women Graduate Students: The Impact of Institutional Factors." *The Community Psychologist* 21: 13-14.

The George Washington University. January 1992. "Sexual Assault/ Rape on Campus Memorandum." Washington, D.C.

Georgia Institute of Technology. 1988. *Sexual Harassment: A Problem You Can Do Something About.* Atlanta: Georgia Institute of Technology.

Goodwin, M.P. Fall 1989. "Sexual Harassment: Experiences of University Employees." *Initiatives: Journal of the National Association for Women Deans, Administrators, and Counselors* 52: 25-33.

Gutek, B.A. August 1981. "Experiences of Sexual Harassment: Results From a Representative Survey." Los Angeles: Paper presented at the American Psychological Association.

Gutek, B.A., and B. Morasch. 1982. "Sex-Ratios, Sex-Role Spillover, and Sexual Harassment of Women at Work." *Journal of Social Issues* 38(4): 55-74.

Hacker, C. 1991. "Sexual Harassment in the Workplace." *Guidepost.* American Association for Counseling and Development.

Hall, G.C.N., R. Hirschman, and L.E. Beutler. 1991. "Introduction to Special Section on Theories of Sexual Aggression." *Journal of Consulting and Clinical Psychology* 59(5): 619-20.

Hamilton, J.A., S.W. Alagna, L.S. King, and C. Lloyd. 1987. "The Emotional Consequences of Gender-Biased Abuse in the Workplace: New Counseling Programs for Sex Discrimination." *Women and Therapy* 6: 155-82.

Helly, D.O. 1987. "Institutional Strategies: Creating a Sexual Harassment Panel." In *Ivory Power: Sexual Harassment on Campus,* edited by M.A. Paludi, 231-50. Albany: State University of New York Press.

Hindus, M. 1990. "Peer Counseling." *Initiatives: Journal of the National Association for Women Deans, Administrators, and Counselors* 52(4): 47.

Hotelling, K. 1991. "Sexual Harassment: A Problem Shielded by Silence." *Journal of Counseling and Development* 69: 497-501.

Howard, S. July/August 1991. "Organizational Resources for Addressing Sexual Harassment." *Journal of Counseling and Development* 69(6): 507-11.

Hughes, J.O., and B.R. Sandler. 1986. *In Case of Sexual Harassment: A Guide for Women Students, We Hope It Doesn't Happen to You, but if It Does . . . .* Booklet published by the Project on the Status of Women. Washington, D.C.: Association of American Colleges. ED 268 920. 9 pp. MF–01; PC–01.

Janoff-Bulman, R., and I.H. Frieze. 1983. "A Theoretical Perspective for Understanding Reactions to Victimization." *Journal of Social Issues* 39: 1-17.

Johnson, R., and G. Schulman. 1989. "Gender-role Composition and Role Entrapment in Decision-Making Groups." *Gender and Society* 3(3): 355-72.

Kanter, R.M. 1977. *Men and Women in the Corporation.* New York: Basic Books.

Keller, E.A. 1988. "Consensual Amorous Relationships Between Faculty and Students: The Constitutional Right to Privacy." *Journal of College and University Law* 15: 21-42.

Kilpatrick, D.G., and L.J. Veronen. 1983. "Treatment of Rape-Related Problems: Crisis Intervention Is Not Enough." In *Crisis Intervention,* edited by L.H. Cohen, W.L. Claiborn, and G.A. Specker, 165-85. New York: Human Sciences Press.

Kilpatrick, D.G., L.J. Veronen, and P.A. Resick. 1982. "Psychological Sequelae to Rape: Assessment and Treatment Strategies." In *Behavioral Medicine: Assessment and Treatment Strategies,* edited by D.M. Doleys, R.L. Meredith, and A.R. Ciminero, 473-98. New York: Plenum Publishing Corporation.

Kirby, D., P. Murrell, and R. Riggs. 1992. "Title IX: The Paper Tiger Gets Teeth." *AGB Reports* 34(8): 23-26.

Kolb, D.A. 1984. *Experiential Learning: Experience as the Source of Learning and Development.* Englewood Cliffs, N.J.: Prentice-Hall.

Koss, M.P. 1990. "Changed Lives: The Psychological Impact of Sexual Harassment." In *Ivory Power: Sexual Harassment on Campus,* edited by M.A. Paludi. Albany: State University of New York Press.

Leatherman, C. December 4, 1991. "Colleges Seek New Ways to Deal With Sexual Harassment as Victims on Campus Are Reluctant to File Complaints." *The Chronicle of Higher Education*: 1.

———. October 14, 1992. "Legacy of a Bitter Sex-Harassment Battle: Rising Complaints, Frustrations, Fears." *The Chronicle of Higher Education*: A17.

Livingston, J.A. 1982. "Responses to Sexual Harassment on the Job: Legal, Organizational, and Individual Actions." *Journal of Social Issues* 38: 5-22.

Lott, B., M.E. Reilly, and D.R. Howard. 1982. "Sexual Assault and Harassment: A Campus Community Case Study." *Signs* 8: 296-319.

Lundberg-Love, P. August 1989. "Clinical Interventions With Victims of Sexual Harassment." New Orleans: Paper presented at the American Psychological Association.

Maihoff, N., and L. Forrest. 1983. "Sexual Harassment in Higher Education: An Assessment Study." *Initiatives: Journal of the National Association of Women Deans, Administrators, and Counselors* 46: 3-8.

McCormick, N., S. Adams-Bohley, S. Peterson, and W. Gaeddert. 1989.

"Sexual Harassment of Students at a Small College." *Initiatives: Journal of the National Association of Women Deans, Administrators, and Counselors* 52(3): 15-23.

McKinney, K., and C. Howard. 1986. "Coerced Intimacy: The Case of Sexual Harassment on a College Campus." Glen Ellyn, Ill.: Paper presented at the annual meeting of the Illinois Sociological Association.

McKinney, K., C. Olson, and A. Satterfield. 1988. "Graduate Students' Perception of and Reaction to Sexual Harassment." *Interpersonal Violence* 3: 319-25.

Memphis State University. Fall 1992. Schedule of Classes.

Minnich, E. 1989. "From the Circle of the Elite to the World of the Whole: Education, Equality, and Excellence." In *Educating the Majority*, edited by C.S. Pearson, D.L. Shavlik, and J.G. Touchton. New York: American Council on Education/Macmillan.

Mooney, C. April 14, 1993. "U. of Virginia Eyes Formally Banning Student-Faculty Sex." *The Chronicle of Higher Education*: A21.

Mulhauser, K. 1992. "Taking a Stand Against Sexual Assault." *AGB Reports* 34(2): 6-11.

National Association for Women in Education. 1992. "Tracking Sexual Harassment Repeat Offenders." *About Women on Campus* 1(2): 5-6.

National Association of College and University Business Officers. 1992. "Human Resources Management." *College and University Business Administration*: 770-71.

National Association of College and University Business Officers. 1992. "Sexual Harassment on Campus." *College and University Business Administration*: 26(9).

National Education Association. 1992. *Sexual Harassment in Higher Education: Concepts and Issues*. Washington D.C.: National Education Association.

Olswang, S. 1992. "Reassessing Effective Procedures in Cases of Sexual Harassment." New Directions for Institutional Research No. 76. San Francisco: Jossey-Bass.

Palmer, P. 1987. "Community, Conflict, and Ways of Knowing." *Change*: 19-20+.

Paludi, M.A., ed. 1990. "The Student in the Back Row: Avoiding Sexual Harassment in the Classroom." In *Ivory Power: Sexual Harassment on Campus*, 281-86. Albany: State University of New York Press.

Paludi, M.A., and R. Barickman, eds. 1991a. "In Their Own Voices: Responses from Individuals Who Have Experienced Sexual Harassment and Supportive Techniques for Dealing With Victims of Sexual Harassment." In *Academic and Workplace Sexual Harassment: A Resource Manual*. Albany: State University of New York Press.

———, eds. 1991b. "Sexual Harassment of Students: Victims of the College Experience." In *Academic and Workplace Sexual Harassment: A Resource Manual*. Albany: State University of New York

Press.

————, eds. 1991c. "Definitions and Incidence of Academic and Workplace Sexual Harassment." In *Academic and Workplace Sexual Harassment: A Resource Manual.* Albany: State University of New York Press.

Project on the Status and Education of Women. 1978. *Sexual Harassment: A Hidden Issue.* Washington, D.C.: Association of American Colleges. ED 157 481. 8 pp. MF–01; PC–01.

Pryor, J.B. 1987. "Sexual Harassment Proclivities in Men." *Roles* 17: 269-89.

Quina, K. 1990. "The Victimization of Women." In *Ivory Power: Sexual Harassment on Campus,* edited by M.A. Paludi. Albany: State University of New York Press.

Rabinowitz, V.C. 1990. "Coping With Sexual Harassment." In *Ivory Power: Sexual Harassment on Campus,* edited by M. A. Paludi. Albany: State University of New York Press.

Rhodes, F.H. 1992. "The Moral Imperative to Prevent Sexual Harassment on Campus." *Initiatives: Journal of the National Association for Women Deans, Administrators, and Counselors:* 1-5.

Riger, S. 1991. "Gender Dilemmas in Sexual Harassment Policies and Procedures." *American Psychologist* 46: 497-505.

Robertson, C., C.C. Dyer, and D.A. Campbell. 1988. "Campus Harassment: Sexual Harassment Policies and Procedures at Institutions of Higher Learning." *Signs* 13: 792-812.

Rowe, M. December 1987. "Taking Control: How to Deal With Harassment." New Haven, Conn.: Speech presented at Yale University.

Russell, S.H., R.S. Cox, C. Williamson, J. Boismier, H. Javitz, and J. Fairweather. 1988. "Faculty in Higher Education Institutions." Washington, D.C.: U. S. Department of Education, Office Educational Research and Improvement. ED 321 628. 209 pp. MF–01; PC–09.

St. Cloud State University. 1992. *Policy Statement on Sexual/Gender Harassment, Sexual Violence, and Racial and Disability Harassment.* St. Cloud, Minn.: St. Cloud State University.

Salisbury, J., A.B. Ginorio, H. Remick, and D.M. Stringer. 1986. "Counseling Victims of Sexual Harassment. Special Issue: Gender Issues in Psychotherapy." *Psychotherapy* 23: 316-24.

Sandler, B.R. 1983. "Writing a Letter to the Sexual Harasser: Another Way of Dealing With the Problem." Paper published by the Project on the Status and Education of Women. Washington, D.C.: American Association of Colleges.

————. December 1986. *The Campus Climate Revisited: Chilly for Women Faculty, Administrators, and Graduate Students.* Washington, D.C.: Project on the Status and Education of Women, Association of American Colleges. ED 298 837. 112 pp. MF–01; PC–05.

————. 1990. "Sexual Harassment: A New Issue for Institutions."

Initiatives: Journal of the National Association for Women Deans, Administrators, and Counselors 52: 5-10.

Schmitz, B. 1992. "Cultural Pluralism and Core Curricula." *Promoting Diversity in College Classrooms: Innovative Responses for the Curriculum, Faculty, and Institutions*, edited by M. Adams. New Directions for Teaching and Learning No. 52. San Francisco: Jossey-Bass.

Schneider, B.E. 1987. "Graduate Women, Sexual Harassment and University Policy." *Journal of Higher Education* 58: 46-65.

Shullman, S. March 1989. "Sexual Harassment: Therapeutic Issues and Interventions." Newport, R.I.: Paper presented at the Association for Women in Psychology.

Southern Association for College Student Affairs Sexual Abuse Task Force. 1990. *Preventing Sexual Harassment and Sexual Assault: A Guidebook for Student Affairs.* Mississippi State University: Southern Association for College Student Affairs.

Stimson, C.R. 1989. "Over-Reaching: Sexual Harassment and Education." *Journal of the National Association for Women Deans and Counselors* 52(3): 1-5.

Sundt, M. 1993. "Effective Sexual Harassment Policies: Focus on the Harasser and the Campus Culture." *Synthesis: Law and Policy in Higher Education* 4(4): 333-34.

Tangri, S.S., M.R. Burt, and L.B. Johnson. 1982. Sexual Harassment at Work: Three Explanatory Models. *Journal of Social Issues* 38(4): 33-54.

Taylor, S.E. 1983. "Adjustment to Threatening Events: A Theory of Cognitive Adaptation." *American Psychologist* 38: 1,161-73.

Till, F.J. 1980. *Sexual Harassment: A Report on the Sexual Harassment of Students.* Washington, D.C.: National Advisory Council on Women's Educational Programs.

U. S. Department of Health, Education, and Welfare. July 21, 1975. *Final Title IX Regulation Implementing Education Amendments of 1972 Prohibiting Sex Discrimination in Education.* Washington, D.C.: U.S. Department of Health, Education, and Welfare, Office for Civil Rights.

Union University. 1992. *Faculty Handbook.* Jackson, Tenn.: Union University.

University of Iowa. 1991. *The University of Iowa Policy on Sexual Harassment and Consensual Relationship.* Iowa City: University of Iowa.

University of South Carolina. 1990. *Sexual Harassment: What It Is, What to Do About It.* Columbia: University of South Carolina.

Vermont State College. 1991. Sexual Harassment Policy. Waterbury: The Board of Trustees of the Vermont State College.

Wagner, K. 1990. "Prevention and Intervention: Developing Campus Policy and Procedures." *Initiatives: Journal of the National Association for Women Deans, Administrators, and Counselors* 52(4): 37-45.

Weddle, C.J. 1992. "The Case for 'Structured Negotiation' in Sexual Misconduct Cases." *Synthesis Law and Policy in Higher Education* 4: 291-92.

Whitmore, R. November 1983. *Sexual Harassment at University of California-Davis.* Davis, Calif.: Women's Resources and Research Center. ED 248 824. 98 pp. MF–01; PC–04.

Williams, E.A., J.A. Lam, and M. Shively. January/February 1992. "The Impact of a University Policy on the Sexual Harassment of Female Students." *Journal of Higher Education* 63(1): 50-64.

Wilson, K.R., and L.A. Kraus. 1983. "Sexual Harassment in the University." *Journal of College Student Personnel* 24: 219-14.

Yale University School of Medicine. 1992. *Tell Someone: Sexual Harassment, Sex Discrimination, Sexism.* New Haven, Conn.: Office for Women in Medicine, Yale University School of Medicine.

Zalk, R., J. Dederich, and M. Paludi. 1991. "Women Students' Assessment of Consensual Relationships With Their Professors: Ivory Power Reconsidered." In *Academic and Workplace Sexual Harassment: A Resource Manual,* edited by M.A. Paludi and R.B. Barickman, 99-111. Albany: State University of New York Press.

Statutes

Cal. [Educ.] Code Sec. 48900.2 (West 1993).

The Campus Sexual Assault Victim's Bill of Rights, 20 U.S.C., Sec. 1092 (1992).

The Civil Rights Act of 1991, 42 U.S.C., Sec. 2000e, et seq. (1992).

The Family Education Rights and Privacy Act of 1974 (The Buckley Amendment), 20 U.S.C. Sec. 1232g (1974).

The Tennessee Human Rights Act, Tenn. Code Ann. Sec. 4-21-101 et seq. (1992).

Title VII of the Civil Rights Act of 1964, 42 U.S.C., Sec. 2000e et seq. (1992).

Title IX of the Education Amendments of 1972, 20 U.S.C., Sec. 1681-1686 (1982).

Uniform Crime Reporting Act, 20 U.S.C., Sec. 1092(f) (1990).

Regulations

29 C.F.R. Sec. 1601.6-1601.29 (1991).

Cases

Andrews v. City of Philadelphia, 895 F.2d 1469 (3d Cir. 1990).

Alexander v. Yale University, 631 F.2d 178 (2d. Cir. 1980).

Barnes v. Costle, 561 F.2d 983 (D.C. Cir. 1977).

Corne v. Bausch & Lomb, Inc., 390 F.Supp. 161 (D.C., Ariz. 1975), vacated and remanded on other grounds, 562 F.2d 55 (9th Cir. 1977).

Ellison v. Bailey, 942 F.2d 872 (9th Cir. 1991).

Franklin v. Gwinnett County Public Schools and Hill, 112 S. Ct. 1028

(1992).

Franklin v. Gwinnett County Public Schools and Hill, 911 F.2d 617 (11th Cir. 1990).

Korf v. Ball State University, 726 F.2d 1222 (7th Cir. 1984).

Levitt v. University of Texas El Paso, 759 F.2d 1224 (5th Cir. 1985).

Lipsett v. University of Puerto Rico, 864 F2d 881 (1st Cir. 1988).

Meritor Savings Bank FSB v. Vinson, 477 U.S. 57, 106 S.Ct. 2399 (1986).

The Red and Black Publishing Co., Inc., et al. v. The Board of Regents et al. 427 S.E.2d 257 (Ga. 1993).

Tomkins v. Public Service Electric and Gas Company, 568 F.2d 1044 (3d. Cir. 1977).

INDEX

A

AASCU. See American Association of State colleges and Universities

AAUP. See American Association of University Professors

accessible grievance procedure, 40-42

ACE. See American Council on Education

Administrators role, 64-66, 70

Alexander v. Yale, 9

Alliance Against Sexual Coercion, 27

American Association of
> State colleges and Universities, 51
> University Professors, 13, 32-33, 42, 50-51

American Council on Education, 13, 35-36, 40, 46, 51

Andrews v. City of Philadelphia, 7

Antioch College, 31, 44

Association of American Colleges, 39, 46

athletics role, 73-74

avoidance response, 21

B

Barnes v. Castle, 5

behavior, v

Buckley Amendment, 45

C

California Sexual Harassment Statutes, 12

Campus Sexual Assault Victims' Bill of Rights, 11-12, 29, 73

Carleton College, 13, 38-39

Center for Health Sciences, University of Tennessee, xvii

Chencharick, Judy, xvii

City University of New York. See Hunter College

Civil Rights Act
> of 1964, 4
> of 1991, 3, 11

classification of sexual harassment. See Fitzgerald et al.

coercion of sexual activity, v, 2, 19

compensatory damages, 11

complaint resolution procedure, 58-62
> confidentiality, 45-46

Consensual Amorous Relationships, 30-34
> forbidden within instructional context, 57
> justification of intimate faculty-student relationship, 30
> suspect between students and faculty, 57-58

Cornell University, 20, 45-46

Crisis
> Consultation Team, 12
> hotline, 28-29
> intervention counseling, 28

cultural standpoint, 23

curriculum role, 70

D
date rape, 20
due process, need for, 47

E
Education, 43-45
Educational
      Amendments of 1972, 3-4, 10, 32
      Programs, 63-64
EEOC. See Equal Employment Opportunity Commission
effective
      communication, 39-40
      goals, 35
effects on the victim, 25-26
Ellison v. Bailey, 7
employer liability guidelines, 7-8
Equal Employment Opportunity Act, 4
Equal Employment Opportunity Commission
      advocacy group, 42
      expanded authority, 4
      guidelines, 2, 5, 6, 7-8, 13
      number of complaints, 3, 18
examples, 55-56

F
Family Educational Rights and Privacy Act of 1974, 45
Fear of Filing a Complaint, 21
Federal Bureau of Investigation, 12
Fitzgerald et al. classification of sexual harassment, 1-2
formal
      action, 62
      complaint, 61-62
forms of discriminatory sexual harassment, 6
Franklin v. Gwinnett, 1, 3, 5, 8-10

G
gender harassment, v, 2, 19
      same as sexual harassment, 1
gender segregation, 68
George Washington University, 12
Georgia Institute of Technology, 37
Governing Boards role, 64-66
grievance procedure accessible. See accessible grievance procedure

H
Hampshire College, 39

Harvard University, 39
Hellman, Ricci, xvii
Hill, Anita, 1
hostile environment, 5-6
        basis for legal claims, 9
Hunter College, 41, 44

I

inappropriate behavior in workplace environment, 14-15
Indiana University, 69
        Office of Womens Affairs, 49
informal resolution procedure, 60-61

K

Korf v. Ball State University, 11
Keller, E. A., 30

L

Lanier, Judge David, 1
letter to harasser, 41, 58
Levitt v. University of Texas, 10-11
Lipsett v. University of Puerto Rico, 7
Louis, Chancellor Kenneth R. R. Gros, 69

M

Massachusetts Institute of Technology, 30
Memphis
        Center for the Study of Higher Education, xvii
        Sexual Abuse Center, xvii
        State University, xvii, 43
Meritor Savings Bank FSB v. Vinson, 2, 5-8, 13
Meritor Applications, 6-8, 32, 35
Michigan State University, 19
Minnesota State University System. See St. Cloud State University
Morris, Pat, xviii

N

NACUBO. See National Association of College & University Business
Officers
National
        Association for Women in Education, 30, 46
        Association of College and University Business Officers,
        51
        Collegiate Athletic Association, 73
        Education Association, 33, 42
natural or biological model, 23-24
NCAA. See National Collegiate Athletic Association
NEA. See National Education Association

Southern Association of College Student Affairs
       guidebook, 72
       Sexual Abuse Task Force, 51-52
student-professor [sexual] experiences.
       See Consensual Amorous Relationships
student services role, 72-73
surveys, 46

T

Tailhook, 1, 67
teaching role, 71-72
Tennesee
       Human Rights Act, 12
       Union University, 38
tenure no protection, 10
third party mediation. See informal resolution procedure
Thomas, Clarence, 1, 3
Tompkins v. Public Service Electric, 5

U

Uniform Crime Reporting System, 12
Union University, xvii
United States
       Merit Systems Protection Board, 48
       Office of Civil Rights, 4, 10
University of
       California at Berkeley, 19
       Iowa, 30-31, 39, 43, 53
       Massachusetts at Amherst, 47-48
       Minnesota, 39
       Pennsylvania, 39
       Rhode Island, 20
       South Carolina, 37
       Tennessee, xvi. See also Center for Health Sciences.
       Virginia, 31-32
       Washington, 49-50

V

verbal harassment, 12
Vermont State College, 31
victims rights, 12

W

Williford, Lucy, xvii
Wilson, Olivia, xvii
Y
Yale University, 9
       School of Medicine, 36

ASHE-ERIC HIGHER EDUCATION REPORTS

Since 1983, the Association for the Study of Higher Education (ASHE) and the Educational Resources Information Center (ERIC) Clearinghouse on Higher Education, a sponsored project of the School of Education and Human Development at The George Washington University, have cosponsored the *ASHE-ERIC Higher Education Report* series. The 1993 series is the twenty-second overall and the fifth to be published by the School of Education and Human Development at the George Washington University.

Each monograph is the definitive analysis of a tough higher education problem, based on thorough research of pertinent literature and institutional experiences. Topics are identified by a national survey. Noted practitioners and scholars are then commissioned to write the reports, with experts providing critical reviews of each manuscript before publication.

Eight monographs (10 before 1985) in the ASHE-ERIC Higher Education Report series are published each year and are available on individual and subscription bases. Subscription to eight issues is $98.00 annually; $78 to members of AAHE, AIR, or AERA; and $68 to ASHE members. All foreign subscribers must include an additional $10 per series year for postage.

To order, use the order form on the last page of this book. Regular prices are as follows:

Series	Price	Series	Price
1993	$18.00	1985 to 87	$10.00
1990 to 92	$17.00	1983 and 84	7.50
1988 and 89	15.00	before 1983	6.50

Discounts on non-subscription orders:
- Bookstores, and current members of AERA, AIR, AAHE and ASHE, receive a 25% discount.
- Bulk: For non-bookstore, non-member orders of 10 or more books, deduct 10%.

Shipping costs are as follows:
- U.S. address: 5% of invoice subtotal for orders over $50.00; $2.50 for each order with an invoice subtotal of $50.00 or less.
- Foreign: $2.50 per book.

All orders under $45.00 must be prepaid. Make check payable to ASHE-ERIC. For Visa or MasterCard, include card number, expiration date and signature.

Address order to
ASHE-ERIC Higher Education Reports
The George Washington University
1 Dupont Circle, Suite 630
Washington, DC 20036
Or phone (202) 296-2597
Write or call for a complete catalog.

1993 ASHE-ERIC Higher Education Reports

1. The Department Chair: New Roles, Responsibilities and Challenges
   Alan T. Seagren, John W. Creswell, and Daniel W. Wheeler

1992 ASHE-ERIC Higher Education Reports

1. The Leadership Compass: Values and Ethics in Higher Education
   John R. Wilcox and Susan L. Ebbs

2. Preparing for a Global Community: Achieving an International Perspective in Higher Education
   Sarah M. Pickert

3. Quality: Transforming Postsecondary Education
   Ellen Earle Chaffee and Lawrence A. Sherr

4. Faculty Job Satisfaction: Women and Minorities in Peril
   Martha Wingard Tack and Carol Logan Patitu

5. Reconciling Rights and Responsibilities of Colleges and Students: Offensive Speech, Assembly, Drug Testing, and Safety
   Annette Gibbs

6. Creating Distinctiveness: Lessons from Uncommon Colleges and Universities
   Barbara K. Townsend, L. Jackson Newell, and Michael D. Wiese

7. Instituting Enduring Innovations: Achieving Continuity of Change in Higher Education
   Barbara K. Curry

8. Crossing Pedagogical Oceans: International Teaching Assistants in U.S. Undergraduate Education
   Rosslyn M. Smith, Patricia Byrd, Gayle L. Nelson, Ralph Pat Barrett, and Janet C. Constantinides

1991 ASHE-ERIC Higher Education Reports

1. Active Learning: Creating Excitement in the Classroom
   Charles C. Bonwell and James A. Eison

2. Realizing Gender Equality in Higher Education: The Need to Integrate Work/Family Issues
   Nancy Hensel

3. Academic Advising for Student Success: A System of Shared Responsibility
   Susan H. Frost

4. Cooperative Learning: Increasing College Faculty Instructional Productivity
   David W. Johnson, Roger T. Johnson, and Karl A. Smith

5. High School–College Partnerships: Conceptual Models, Programs, and Issues
   Arthur Richard Greenberg

6. Meeting the Mandate: Renewing the College and Departmental Curriculum
   William Toombs and William Tierney

7. Faculty Collaboration: Enhancing the Quality of Scholarship and Teaching
   Ann E. Austin and Roger G. Baldwin

8. Strategies and Consequences: Managing the Costs in Higher Education
   John S. Waggaman

1990 ASHE-ERIC Higher Education Reports

1. The Campus Green: Fund Raising in Higher Education
   Barbara E. Brittingham and Thomas R. Pezzullo

2. The Emeritus Professor: Old Rank - New Meaning
   James E. Mauch, Jack W. Birch, and Jack Matthews

3. "High Risk" Students in Higher Education: Future Trends
   Dionne J. Jones and Betty Collier Watson

4. Budgeting for Higher Education at the State Level: Enigma, Paradox, and Ritual
   Daniel T. Layzell and Jan W. Lyddon

5. Proprietary Schools: Programs, Policies, and Prospects
   John B. Lee and Jamie P. Merisotis

6. College Choice: Understanding Student Enrollment Behavior
   Michael B. Paulsen

7. Pursuing Diversity: Recruiting College Minority Students
   Barbara Astone and Elsa Nuñez-Wormack

8. Social Consciousness and Career Awareness: Emerging Link in Higher Education
   John S. Swift, Jr.

1989 ASHE-ERIC Higher Education Reports

1. Making Sense of Administrative Leadership: The 'L' Word in Higher Education
   Estela M. Bensimon, Anna Neumann, and Robert Birnbaum

2. Affirmative Rhetoric, Negative Action: African-American and Hispanic Faculty at Predominantly White Universities
   Valora Washington and William Harvey

3. Postsecondary Developmental Programs: A Traditional Agenda with New Imperatives
   Louise M. Tomlinson

4. The Old College Try: Balancing Athletics and Academics in Higher Education
   John R. Thelin and Lawrence L. Wiseman

5. The Challenge of Diversity: Involvement or Alienation in the Academy?
   Daryl G. Smith

6. Student Goals for College and Courses: A Missing Link in Assessing and Improving Academic Achievement
   Joan S. Stark, Kathleen M. Shaw, and Malcolm A. Lowther

7. The Student as Commuter: Developing a Comprehensive Institutional Response
   Barbara Jacoby

8. Renewing Civic Capacity: Preparing College Students for Service and Citizenship
   Suzanne W. Morse

1988 ASHE-ERIC Higher Education Reports

1. The Invisible Tapestry: Culture in American Colleges and Universities
   George D. Kuh and Elizabeth J. Whitt

2. Critical Thinking: Theory, Research, Practice, and Possibilities
   Joanne Gainen Kurfiss

3. Developing Academic Programs: The Climate for Innovation
   Daniel T. Seymour

4. Peer Teaching: To Teach is To Learn Twice
   Neal A. Whitman

5. Higher Education and State Governments: Renewed Partnership, Cooperation, or Competition?
   Edward R. Hines

6. Entrepreneurship and Higher Education: Lessons for Colleges, Universities, and Industry
   James S. Fairweather

7. Planning for Microcomputers in Higher Education: Strategies for the Next Generation
   Reynolds Ferrante, John Hayman, Mary Susan Carlson, and Harry Phillips

8. The Challenge for Research in Higher Education: Harmonizing Excellence and Utility
   Alan W. Lindsay and Ruth T. Neumann

1987 ASHE-ERIC Higher Education Reports

1. Incentive Early Retirement Programs for Faculty: Innovative Responses to a Changing Environment
   Jay L. Chronister and Thomas R. Kepple, Jr.

2. Working Effectively with Trustees: Building Cooperative Campus Leadership
   Barbara E. Taylor

3. Formal Recognition of Employer-Sponsored Instruction: Conflict and Collegiality in Postsecondary Education
   Nancy S. Nash and Elizabeth M. Hawthorne

4. Learning Styles: Implications for Improving Educational Practices
   Charles S. Claxton and Patricia H. Murrell

5. Higher Education Leadership: Enhancing Skills through Professional Development Programs
   Sharon A. McDade

6. Higher Education and the Public Trust: Improving Stature in Colleges and Universities
   Richard L. Alfred and Julie Weissman

7. College Student Outcomes Assessment: A Talent Development Perspective
   Maryann Jacobi, Alexander Astin, and Frank Ayala, Jr.

8. Opportunity from Strength: Strategic Planning Clarified with Case Examples
   Robert G. Cope

1986 ASHE-ERIC Higher Education Reports

1. Post-tenure Faculty Evaluation: Threat or Opportunity?
   Christine M. Licata

2. Blue Ribbon Commissions and Higher Education: Changing Academe from the Outside
   Janet R. Johnson and Laurence R. Marcus

3. Responsive Professional Education: Balancing Outcomes and Opportunities
   Joan S. Stark, Malcolm A. Lowther, and Bonnie M.K. Hagerty

4. Increasing Students' Learning: A Faculty Guide to Reducing Stress among Students
   Neal A. Whitman, David C. Spendlove, and Claire H. Clark

5. Student Financial Aid and Women: Equity Dilemma?
   Mary Moran

6. The Master's Degree: Tradition, Diversity, Innovation
   Judith S. Glazer

*Out-of-print. Available through EDRS. Call 1-800-443-ERIC.

ORDER FORM

Quantity   **Amount**

_____ Please begin my subscription to the 1993 *ASHE-ERIC Higher Education Reports* at $98.00, 32% off the cover price, starting with Report 1, 1993.   _____

_____ Please send a complete set of the 1992 *ASHE-ERIC Higher Education Reports* at $90.00, 33% off the cover price.   _____

_____ Outside the U.S., add $10.00 per series for postage.   _____

Individual reports are avilable at the following prices:

1993, $18.00	1985 to 1987, $10.00
1990 to 1992, $17.00	1983 and 1984, $7.50
1988 and 1989, $15.00	1980 to 1982, $6.50

SHIPPING: **U.S. Orders:** *For subtotal (before discount) of $50.00 or less, add $2.50. For subtotal over $50.00, add 5% of subtotal. Call for rush service options.* **Foreign Orders:** *$2.50 per book.* **U.S. Subscriptions:** *Included in price.* **Foreign Subscriptions:** *Add $10.00*

PLEASE SEND ME THE FOLLOWING REPORTS:

Quantity	Report No.	Year	Title	Amount

Subtotal:	
Shipping:	
Total Due:	

Please check one of the following:
- ☐ Check enclosed, payable to GWU–ERIC.
- ☐ Purchase order attached ($45.00 minimum).
- ☐ Charge my credit card indicated below:
  - ☐ Visa   ☐ MasterCard

Expiration Date _____

Name _____

Title _____

Institution _____

Address _____

City _____ State _____ Zip _____

Phone _____ Fax _____ Telex _____

Signature _____ Date _____

SEND ALL ORDERS TO:
ASHE-ERIC Higher Education Reports
The George Washington University
One Dupont Circle, Suite 630
Washington, DC 20036-1183
Phone: (202) 296-2597

370.19345 Rig
Riggs, Robert O.
Sexual harassment in higher
  education